GLOBAL CHALLENGE
TO THE
UNITED STATES

GLOBAL
CHALLENGE
TO THE
UNITED STATES

A study of the problems, the perils,
and the proposed solutions involved
in Washington's search for a new
role in the world

Summary and Analysis

by LESTER MARKEL and AUDREY MARCH

RUTHERFORD • MADISON • TEANECK
FAIRLEIGH DICKINSON UNIVERSITY PRESS
LONDON: ASSOCIATED UNIVERSITY PRESSES

© 1976 by Associated University Presses Inc.

Associated University Presses, Inc.
Cranbury, New Jersey 08512

Associated University Presses
108 New Bond Street
London W1Y OQX, England

Library of Congress Cataloging in Publication Data
Main entry under title:

Global challenge to the United States.

(The Leverton lecture series)
Report on a project conducted by the Graduate Institute of
International Studies at Fairleigh Dickinson University.
1. United States—Foreign relations—1945—I. Markel, Lester,
1894—   II. March, Audrey.   III. Fairleigh Dickinson Uni-
versity. Graduate Institute of International Studies.   IV. Series.
JX1417.G57   327.73   75—18807
ISBN 0–8386–1822–7

CONTENTS

ABOUT THE BOOK

This project was conceived and directed by Lester Markel, former Sunday Editor of the *New York Times* and Visiting Professor at Fairleigh Dickinson's Graduate Institute of International Studies. He also acted as moderator of the panels. The report is the joint work of Mr. Markel and Mrs. Audrey March, political analyst, who assisted Mr. Markel throughout the project.

Mr. Markel herewith expresses his gratitude to Mrs. March; to Dr. Nasrollah Fatemi, who facilitated the project; to Ann and Morris Leverton, whose gift made possible the Leverton series of lectures that formed part of this study; and to the *New York Times* and the *Bergen Record,* who supplied funds for much of the research.

FOREWORD

This is the first publication resulting from the Leverton lecture and panel series conducted at the Teaneck Campus of Fairleigh Dickinson University. This volume deals with one of the most critical problems facing the United States: the creation of a new foreign policy for a new kind of world. Our hope is that the conclusions and suggestions presented in this study will not only benefit the public but also assist policy makers in their deliberations.

The project was unique in that it combined the three techniques; in addition to the lectures, panels and research, questionnaires, submitted in person and by mail, brought almost a hundred expert comments. The book is also unique in that it is not the usual reprint of speeches, published chronologically and without relationship to one another; rather, it is arranged by subject, so that the viewpoints on any particular issue are presented in unified sequence. I commend Mr. Markel and Mrs. March for the breadth and illumination of this work.

The Leverton lecture series was made possible by the generous grant of Ann and Morris Leverton. Dr. Leverton, a financier-philanthropist (and Chairman of the Leverton Lecture Series Teaneck), has been a member of the Board of Fellows at Fairleigh Dickinson University for the last ten years. He has served as the representative of the University's Board of Overseers to Wroxton College, FDU's campus in England. His support of and interest in the development of Wroxton College and the Graduate Institute of International Studies at FDU have been a source of encouragement and strength and are tremendously appreciated.

Nasrollah S. Fatemi

INTRODUCTION

This is a report on a project that deals with a problem as challenging as any in the nation's history—a study of this question: How can we find a new and effective role in this world of revolutionary change?

Over a period of two years, at the Graduate Institute of International Studies at Fairleigh Dickinson University, various aspects of the problem have been explored by students and outside researchers. The findings reveal both dangers and opportunities, the rigors of the task and the imagination and education needed to overcome them.

The background of the last thirty years, during which the world was transformed, points up the complexity and the proportions of the effort. The foreign policy that served us through two world wars is outdated and no longer relevant. That policy was based on the concept that the United States, without doubt, was the number-one nation. But the rise of other nations and new global tides have altered our world status and compelled us to search out a new course.

The soundness and success of a new policy depend large-ly on two elements—strong leadership and informed public opinion. These two forces are likely to determine whether we shall live in a world of hope or of despair. If we are to ensure liberty and the chance to pursue happiness, heroic measures are needed.

* * * *

The program was an extensive one—interviews with members of the Executive offices, the State Department, and the Congress; talks with public and private citizens; inquiries into government and media performance in the area of public opinion.

An important and illuminating part of the project was a series of twenty panels, held under the auspices of the University, in which experts from the media, the academic world, the government, and the public considered the problems involved in the survey. A valuable contribution was a series of mail interviews, with comments from close to one hundred public citizens.

In the course of the discussions a great deal of ancillary material was developed—including material of interest in the coming Presidential election; light on the Presidency, on the Congress, and on the voter; the qualities of leadership; the importance of TV charisma; and so forth. And there were debates over such questions as the part Congress plays in foreign policy, the importance of domestic feeling about foreign issues, programs for a revolution in education.

* * * *

The presentation is in five parts:

Part I: "The Global Crisis"—the highlights and the implications of the problems of the new world order, with emphasis on the task of the United States.

Part II: "The Ideal Leader"—the qualities required of a President in these critical and crowded days and an analysis of present and past presidential performances.

Part III: "Opinion"—or Emotion?—the need of developing a public opinion in foreign policy; a profile of the voter and an appraisal of the forces that operate on him, with emphasis on the media.

Part IV: "Tests For Democracy"—a discussion of whether under these new stresses we are neglecting our fundamental effort; a symposium on what is our paramount problem.

Part V: "Conclusion and Commentary"—a summing up by the editors of the main points of the survey and a statement of optimism or pessimism.

* * * *

These are the outstanding findings:

Internationally

1. This is beyond the shadow of a doubt an interdependent world; no nation is an island unto itself.

2. An unprecedented situation confronts us. As Henry Kissinger says: "The first truly world crisis is that which we now face. It requires the first truly global solutions."

3. First in international importance are the problems of human distress—overpopulation, poverty, hunger, pollution —the problems of the Third World. Mankind cannot exist one-third "have" and two-thirds "have not."

4. Unless the armaments race is halted, there will not be the resources to remedy the social ills that plague the world, even the "have" nations.

5. Communication among nations must be improved, so that there will be no false images and no baseless rumors; understanding is an essential key to peace.

Nationally

1. The days of isolation are gone. We are part of the world and we cannot escape our responsibility.

2. We must find a new foreign policy, one based on co-operation rather than confrontation, on agreement rather than muscle.

3. The public has scant information about foreign affairs and makes little effort to understand them, because it does not seem to realize that domestic policy and foreign policy cannot be separated.

4. Leadership is essential to persuade the Congress and the people of the need of this new policy.

5. The President, the Congress, the media, all the forces of education must adopt new programs designed to inform public opinion.

At this point, an inquiring reader may rise and ask: "And how does it leave you editors—optimistic or pessimistic?" The answer is "with restrained optimism."

*   *   *   *

The quotations are taken from the questionnaires, the interviews, the panels, and the readings. Any unquoted text was supplied by the editors. The appendix contains the answers to the various questionnaires; it will be found to be, we feel, of considerable interest both because of the standing of the respondents and the quality of their replies.

THOSE QUOTED IN THE TEXT

Ben Bagdikian, author and media critic
Thomas Bailey, Professor of History, Stanford University
Benjamin Bradlee, Executive Editor, *Washington Post*
Zbigniew Brzezinski, Director, Research Institute on International Change, Columbia University
J. Herbert Burke, member of Congress
James McGregor Burns, Professor of Political Science, Williams College
Ruth Clark, Vice-President, Yankelovich, Skelly and White
William Crotty, Professor of Political Science, Northwestern University
W. Phillips Davison, Professor, Graduate School of Journalism, Columbia University

Nasrollah S. Fatemi, Director, Graduate Institute of International Studies, Fairleigh Dickinson University

Charles Frankel, Professor of Philosophy and Public Affairs, Columbia University

Betty Friedan, author, founder of National Organization for Women

Wes Gallagher, President and General Manager, Associated Press

George Gallup, Director, American Institute of Public Opinion

Doris Graber, Professor of Political Science, University of Illinois

Henry Graff, Professor of History, Columbia University

Peter Grose, member, editorial board, *New York Times*

Paul Hollander, Professor of Sociology, University of Massachusetts

Pat M. Holt, Chief of Staff, Senate Committee on Foreign Relations

Sidney Hyman, historian and Professor of Political Science, University of Chicago

Nicholas Katzenbach, General Counsel, International Business Machines

Henry Kissinger, Secretary of State

Robert Kleiman, member, editorial board, *New York Times*

Wilbur Landrey, Foreign Editor, United Press International

Paul F. Lazarsfeld, Chairman, Columbia Bureau of Applied Social Research, Columbia University

Anthony Lewis, columnist, *New York Times*

Marya Mannes, author

David MacEachron, Executive Director, Japan Society

Drew Middleton, military correspondent, *New York Times*

Akira Nagata, General Manager, American District, *Nihon Economic Journal*

Michael O'Neill, Editor, *New York Daily News*

Ithiel de Sola Pool, Professor of Political Science, Massachusetts Institute of Technology

George Reedy, Dean, College of Journalism, Marquette University

Dean Rusk, Professor of Law, University of Georgia

Harrison Salisbury, former Associate Editor and Op Ed Page Editor, *New York Times*

Robert Semple, Chief, London Bureau, *New York Times*

Gemmadiy Shishkin, Manager, Tass Agency, New York City

Stanley M. Swinton, Vice-President and Assistant General Manager, Associated Press

Audrey Topping, authority on China

David Truman, President, Mount Holyoke College

Alfred von Krusenstiern, Bureau Chief, Springer Foreign News Service

David Webster, Director, U.S. Office of the British Broadcasting Company

Thomas G. Wicker, columnist, *New York Times*

Daniel Yankelovich, President, Yankelovich, Skelly and White

PART I:
THE GLOBAL CRISIS

The report begins with the background—a survey of the world changes since World War II, a statement of the reasons why the old policy no longer is pertinent or possible and an indication of the difficulties of the search.

Chapter 1
THIRTY FATEFUL YEARS

The three decades since the end of World War II form as dramatic a period as any in the world's history, with no change more dramatic than the alteration in the role of the United States. A comparison of the world of 1945 with the world of today illuminates the almost incredible transformation:

1945—Europe was in chaos, its industrial plant wrecked by the war, its social life utterly disrupted. The Soviet Union was showing signs of aggression, but it was a devastated land and recovery seemed far off. China was wracked by civil war; Japan was searching painfully for hope in the atomic debris. The United States had colossal strength in those years. Our policy was world policy, and for two decades it was dominated by a single objective—to contain Communism.

1975—Western Europe is able to compete economically with the United States; the dependence on us is ended. The Soviet Union, armed with nuclear weaponry and her plants restored, is a potent military power. China, too, has nuclear weapons and strong leadership, even though she lags industrially. Japan has demonstrated her enormous capability. As for us, we are no longer the undisputed power. Vietnam revealed our vulnerability; our self-assurance is gone. Although we are stronger today, even with our spiritual weakness, than we were at the end of World War II, relatively we are less powerful.

What had happened in those three decades? Recovery in many countries, assertions of independence, the raising of voices at times more persuasive than that of the United States. But there were new and disturbing elements also. Signs of difficulties in the world economy began to appear. The seeds sown in the two World Wars—dragon seeds they surely were—had been sprouting during the thirty-year period. One by one the European empires collapsed—England's, France's, Belgium's.

Even though Africa has been completely transformed, she remains the dark continent. In 1945 there were only four independent nations on all the continent; a quarter of a century later there are more than forty. These new governments soon found themselves beset with political, economic, and social problems, plus epidemics of tribalism and racism. The problems are compounded by a population increase; world population, which stood at about 2½ billion in '45, has grown at the rate of 75 million a year until now the total is four billion. And it has increased most rapidly in Africa, Asia, and Latin America, areas with limited resources and unlimited poverty.

In the two decades following the war, our primary policy was to counter what we saw as the growing threat from the Soviet Union. Accordingly, we adopted a threefold program: containment of Communism, deterrence of Soviet military might, and economic support for our allies and new associates. We created the Marshall Plan, the Truman Doctrine, NATO, and a score of military and economic assistance plans for developing nations.

Then Came Vietnam

But for twenty years we had paid scant attention to the new facts of international life. In our confidence in our stability and in our self-congratulation that we were the most generous nation in history, we virtually ignored what had happened in the rest of the world. Then came Vietnam and the worldwide economic crisis, and we were engulfed too. Only then did we renounce the crusading motif. The slow and painful path toward recognition of reality is described by Mr. Salisbury:

"The Wilsonian view was an illusion that continued to influence ideas about American foreign policy as we went into World War II, and, after the defeat of Germany and Japan, most Americans felt that we had indeed made the world safe for democracy. The truth is that we had done nothing of the kind. In fact, although we did not perceive it, we had probably made the world safe for the growth of military dictatorships and undemocratic regimes.

"Vietnam finally made us realize how naive the Wilsonian concept was. The national mood has become one of retreat from as many foreign commitments as possible."

Two other factors affect America's ability to influence world affairs: the concept of relative strength and the realization that we are dependent on other countries for certain materials without which our economy cannot function.

Thus it was not until the third decade after World War II that we finally realized that we were overextended and had fallen victim to what Nicholas Katzenbach calls the "bloated concept of national security." At the same time, the Russians began to make friendly gestures and to soft-pedal the cold war—all this while we were bogged down in Southeast Asia. So we decided the old policy would not do and the search began for a new formula—which is our present endeavor.

The Kissinger Formula

Mr. McEachron describes the mood: "When President Nixon came into office he sensed that the nation was fed up with what seemed like an endless war in Vietnam and with endless foreign aid programs that did not seem to have many good results. Foreign aid had become a favorite whipping-boy in Congress.

"The President recognized that we were overextended, not so much in physical terms but in the way everybody was feeling, and that we had to have some retrenchment. We would continue to provide a nuclear shield for nations and we would help those who helped themselves, but we would never commit ground forces again.

"I think in general the new doctrine is a loose sort of notion that we're somehow going to do less in the world than we've done before. All of these things indicate that the government recognizes a mood of withdrawal on the part of the people.

"Insofar as it has a philosophical foundation, I think it's what Henry Kissinger conceived. As I understand it, it's largely the idea that we will be the swing power of the world, the balancers, assuming somewhat the same role the

British thought they were playing in the last century. The underlying notion seems to be that we will be friendly to both Russia and China and, in doing so, keep them both nervous; and to make Japan and Western Europe more independent.

"Even though Kissinger has retreated precipitously from this language about five powers with the United States as the balancing power, I think there really is a great deal of the nineteenth-century balance-of-power philosophy in his thinking."

Our policy cannot yet be exactly described. It is certainly not Wilsonian idealism or Dulles muscle-flexing; it aims to substitute cooperation for competition and international for national policy. But the details are vague, as vague as the world picture.

There are those who question the current trend, among them Mr. Lewis, who observed:

"I would say that one of the problems of the Kissinger policy is that of priorities. In hindsight, which is always a little unfair, it seems to me that the priorities are wrong. Henry Kissinger spent four years—and that's an awfully long time—in secret negotiations over Vietnam, while those other matters we talk about—the world economic situation, for example, or our relationship with our allies—didn't interest him.

"The trouble with our foreign policy for quite a long time has been that we have concentrated on things that, relatively speaking, aren't important. Today the most important things in the world are the issues of overpopulation and mass starvation. . . . Meanwhile our foreign-policy experts and our foreign-policy machinery have been involved—I'm sorry to use the same example, but it happens to be the one in which we spent our effort for so many years—in an irrelevance like supporting Nguyen Van Thieu as President of South Vietnam."

The Issue of Morality

These remarks made during a panel discussion led into a fascinating debate over the "morality" of our foreign policy. This is Mr. MacEachron's view:

"The world cannot be made safe for democracy by war, nor can it be done in one generation. Democracy, as we know, is a very difficult form of government, and making the whole world safe for democracy will take centuries, not decades. Meanwhile we often have to compromise. As Churchill said, in war one has to make peace with the devil to fight the enemy. But I do think that because this country is a democracy and because we're all imbued, whether we like to admit it or not, with a deeply moral sense, it's very difficult for Americans to be honest-to-goodness, effective Machiavellians. And whenever we try (as in the Bay of Pigs, for example) we make a botch of it.

"What we have to do instead is try to build economic and political institutions and, with other nations, gradually recognize certain legal and moral constraints that in fact will make it a safer world for us to live in. I defend the effort to make the world safe for democracy."

Mr. Lewis said he was "really on that side of the argument, because I believe that Machiavellianism is unsatisfactory as a policy for this country. I think we do, all of us, long for some nobler objective than self-interest. But I have difficulty reconciling that with one exception which I'm afraid can't be avoided, and that is Vietnam. I cannot find any noble objective for our being there, although maybe there was at the beginning. As it went on—certainly for the last four years—there was no logical basis for our being there except that it would have been politically damaging for us to have pulled out. There couldn't be a more cynical reason for destroying a country thousands of miles away. And that is what I find hard to square with what I believe are the instincts and the natural tendencies of this country.

"This issue of morality shows up clearly when it is considered in the American-Soviet context. If, for example, Solzhenitsyn, instead of being exiled, had been—let's take the extreme case—sentenced to death, should that sort of thing have disrupted the American-Soviet relationship? As a purely practical matter, one can say that no matter what happens to Solzhenitsyn, it's still desirable to work out arms controls and economic arrangements, and yet I can't bring myself to believe that we should not be concerned about the other issue."

Dr. Fatemi agreed. "I always think of what would have happened if in 1934 or 1935 the United States, England, France, and the Vatican had told Hitler to stop what he was doing or they would break diplomatic and economic relations with him. According to all the information we have, Hitler would have been overthrown by his own generals, and we would have had a very different world. The trouble is, however, that foreign policy must be made in the national interest.

"When William Pitt was asked what the foreign policy of England should be, he said that the first question that had to be asked was: Is it a moral foreign policy, in the sense that one could say that England was fighting for a principle? The second question was: Is it in the national interest? The third question was: How much would it cost? The fourth was: Could England afford it? And the last was: Even if the country could afford it, was it worth it?

"I think there has to be some sort of consistency to foreign policy if we expect the people to support it. I think this is what went wrong in Vietnam. It could never be sold to the American public. There was no moral reason for it."

Morality—"Not A Bit"

Mr. Salisbury dissented: "I think that our foreign policy today is based on complete cynicism, and on balance of power. I don't think you'll find an ounce of genuine morality in it anywhere. Now George Kennan has long argued a very good case for eliminating morality from foreign policy. I myself find it a very difficult thing to do and I think most Americans do too.

"The Kennan argument has always been that foreign policy is based on national interest, but that it is usually well-larded and buttered up with pseudo-morality. If we go to war, it's always for the most just of causes, as in the case of Vietnam. In this, of course, we're no different from any other nation. No nation goes to war except for the most holy of purposes.

"I believe that if we single out each element of the policy we are following today, we'll find that there isn't any morality in our dealings with the Soviet Union. What there is, however, is a balance-of-power purpose—an effort to establish a stable balance between two great states which are capable of destroying each other. In one way or another, each state is groping for that kind of solution.

"I don't think there's any morality on the Soviet side, and I don't think there's any on the American side. I think there's a good deal of stupidity on the American side, more than is generally conceded, and a generous amount on the Soviet side as well. I don't think there was any morality involved in our policy vis-à-vis China. It was pure balance of power, aimed at creating a larger area of stability in the world, and, from that standpoint, it wasn't badly designed."

The debate ended on this inconclusive note: our role for the future could not be discerned for the cosmic clouds.

Was there hope? Did the fact that we were no longer the supreme nation mean we were to be assigned a lesser role? Dr. Fatemi's answer was this:

"The United States is still a strong nation. If you ask, however, if the leadership is strong, the answer is no. There are three aspects of national strength—political, economic, and military. It is the political factor that has become weak in the United States. If the people of a nation believe in their government, then there is a strong domestic base; and if there is a strong domestic base, there is likely to be a strong foreign policy.

"As for our economic position, I do not think that any country on earth has ever had better potential. Western Europe and Japan may be strong in industrial production, but they lack raw materials. The United States is strong in both industrial and agricultural production. We have eight hundred million acres of arable land, and in 1972 only two hundred million of these acres were planted."

Mr. Lewis had a reservation: "I see the current situation a little more ambivalently. For one thing, while it is true that today we are the country that most powerfully combines natural resources and technological achievement, it is also true that we have become more dependent economically on the rest of the world."

*   *   *   *

It is then an interdependent as well as an unsettled world to which the United States must adjust itself. And there are many and complex questions that must be answered, as the following chapter reveals.

Chapter 2
WORLD PUZZLES

The world has become so complex and its problems so magnified that our search for a new foreign policy is a giant puzzle. The issues with which we must deal range from nuclear competition with the Soviet Union to tribal conflicts within small African states, from international monetary programs to food supplies for drought-ridden nations.

The problems of the world are America's problems and vice versa; as Secretary of State Kissinger points out: "The world has become interdependent in economics, in communications, in human aspirations. No one nation, no one part of the world, can prosper or be secure in isolation. . . . For America, involvement in world affairs is no longer an act of choice but the expression of a reality. When weapons span continents in minutes, our security is bound up with world security. When our factories and farms and our financial strength are so closely linked with those of other countries and peoples, our prosperity is tied to world prosperity."

The international crises that confront us are of two kinds: conflicts and confrontations involving specific countries and areas (call them "inter-nation" problems) and situations that transcend national concerns and are global in scope (international problems).

Consider first the nation and area problems. The negotiations with Russia involve, in addition to political and geographic issues, the basic question of armaments—the amount of money we must spend on defense, which in turn directly affects the size of our national debt and the state of our consumer economy.

Another problem in this area is the political and economic viability of our European allies. An abiding concern of our foreign-policy makers since the days of the Marshall Plan has been the fostering of economic cooperation among our NATO allies, with the hope that political and military coordination would follow. But today harmony among the nations of Western Europe is not easily achieved. France, in particular, seeks to make her own economic arrangements with the rest of the world without consultation with the other Common Market countries; Italy seems on the verge of financial collapse; Greece and Turkey are engaged in a bitter debate over Cyprus; Great Britain has reaffirmed her support of the Common Market, but terms must still be arranged.

All our European allies are threatened by inflation and by the skyrocketing costs of energy. We are concerned about these problems because at a time when our own economy is suffering from inflation and a large trade deficit, a significant part of our budget is devoted to the defense of Western Europe.

Our relationship with Tokyo presents a third problem. Although we are committed to provide a nuclear shield for Japan, we feel that trade arrangements made in the post-World War II years to aid Japanese economic growth are no longer justified at a time when Japan's industries compete so extensively with our own.

Southeast Asia is still an unresolved dilemma. The crisis did not disappear with our disengagement from Vietnam; it still cuts into our financial resources and divides us politically.

In the United Nations the burgeoning new nations of Africa bitterly condemn American policy and we are finally beginning to realize the importance of these long-neglected areas.

The Middle East problem involved much more than the conflict between the Arabs and the Israelis because of Soviet-American competition there. Our policy has been to negotiate separately with the opponents, but Russia holds the key to any settlement, since it is Soviet tanks and Soviet missiles that face the Israelies in the Sinai.

Finally there is the riddle of our relationship with the People's Republic of China. After twenty-five years of bitter enmity, nonrecognition, and nonnegotiation, what is to be our policy toward that nation, which contains one-third of the population of the world? Moreover, any normalization of ties necessitates some decision about Taiwan, whose sovereignty we have guaranteed for two-and-a-half decades.

Central Issue: Moscow

Of these problems involving our relationship with individual nations, the paramount one is the negotiation with Russia. The important question about Moscow is whether we can, for practical reasons, or should, for ideological reasons, arrange a détente with a nation whose repressive internal policies repel us and whose defense establishment threatens us.

Mr. Grose, when asked if he thought it possible for the United States to work out a policy of cooperation with a totalitarian society, replied that the basic issue was not the possibility of reduced tensions with a police state, but rather this question: "Will a reduction of tensions between a democracy and a totalitarian regime promote the internal liberalization of the police state?"

Mr. Grose answered his own question: "To start off with," he said, "I would draw a sharp distinction which has been slurred over in the discussion of détente. There is a vast difference between the reduction of tensions among nations and the reduction of tensions with a nation. To argue that détente in Soviet-American relations will bring democratization of Soviet society has no logical basis. Our history is full of examples of warm relations with countries that are veritable police states."

Mr. Grose added, however, that this was a wide-open debate: "We could line up experts on both sides of the room, and they'd be arguing the point until next November."

But how about the fact that both sides are building up their military strength? Dr. Hollander commented: "It is very important to recognize that the two sides are not increasing their armaments at the same rate. The Soviet Union is building with far greater intensity than we are. Soviet armed forces are being expanded, modernized and equipped with advanced weapons which the American armed forces apparently do not have. And the Russians have no problems with public opinion or with congressmen who tell them that more housing is needed rather than a more advanced type of fighter bomber or better submarine-detection devices. The armaments deadlock casts doubt on the genuineness of the Soviet desire for détente or, as it used to be called, peaceful coexistence."

In addition to military competition, there is the problem of ideological disputes. Dr. Hollander pointed out that "the Soviet Union for almost twenty years has consistently emphasized that whatever happens in the realm of foreign policy, the ideological struggle will continue. And the unfavorable picture the Russians paint of the United States has not significantly changed over this period of 'peaceful coexistence.' Moreover, the Russians claim that we want détente because the forces of imperialism, and primarily the United States, are now weaker. And they are right. We are weaker."

What Is the Prospect?

What then is the hope of accommodation? How do we achieve détente? What is the objective of our new policy? Mr. Kleiman believes that "the aim of the Kissinger foreign policy has been the creation of a web of interests between the United States and the Soviet Union. The idea is that we become mutually dependent. If the Soviet Union relies on American grain and the United States relies on Soviet gas, we will be less inclined to risk this dependence. If the Soviet Union should ever be totally self-sufficient, it would likely be more irresponsible than if further development depended on maintaining equilibrium in international relations."

In the light of the suspicion about Soviet military and ideological policies and the fact that freedom of speech is repressed in Russia, Mr. Kleiman was asked how it might be possible to create such a "vested interest in peace." He said that "there are now people who are part of the Soviet establishment who are discontented with the way their society operates. They do not directly challenge the Soviet system, but they do challenge the way in which it functions.

"This type of discussion within the Soviet Union is new; it is taking place in institutions, in industry, and, to a lesser extent, in agriculture. While a Western type of liberalization or democracy is not evolving in the Soviet Union, there are the beginnings of questioning and the growth of groups with an interest in relations with the outside world. While we should not exaggerate these developments, they are of some importance."

The question arose as to what reasons the Soviet Union has for promoting détente. Mr. Salisbury commented: "Of all the problems which the Russians face, the most difficult to resolve, given the present leadership and existing system, are the domestic issues. The success or failure of any government, whether or not it has a Kissinger at its head, rests on the handling of domestic problems. If you can't solve them, your foreign policy dissipates.

"The Russians' external policy at this time is strongly conditioned by internal problems. Their effort to get technical and material aid from the United States, their capitalist competitor, the epitome of evil, is an attempt to infuse their dead economy somehow and enable them to meet the increasing demands of their people. The rising expectations which have been fed to the people by their leadership are becoming harder to fulfill and more dangerous, because the great masses may one day turn on the frightened men in the Kremlin and throw them out. And so the Soviet leaders are engaged in a great flirtation with the United States because, realizing that they need what we have, they have tried everything else. They have tried the police; they have experimented with the carrot, with the stick, and with various other devices; but as long as they are saddled with an archaic bureaucracy, they cannot make industry and agriculture work. And that is why trade and technological aid from us is so strong an objective of their foreign policy. They hope it will save their skins as well as their country.

"The other and greatest worry of the Russian leaders is China. They see China as an enormous, irrational power about to attack them at almost any time across the common 4,500-mile frontier or, if not now, as soon as they are strong enough. The Russians are told by their 'Pentagon,' which I suspect is even more powerful than ours, that the way to deal with the Chinese is to halt them before they become too strong to handle."

Such, then, are the "inter-nation" problems—delicate and complex. We come now to the second category of problems—those of global scope, of even longer range and deeper meaning than the first group, because sooner or later they will affect us all.

Of these problems, the two that have precedence are the plight of the Third World and the international economy. In a sense both are economic in nature. They include wretched poverty and the unequal distribution of resources among nations; a population explosion in the underdeveloped countries that can least afford more mouths to feed; the dwindling supply of essential resources; pollution of the atmosphere and oceans; and worldwide inflation that threatens to weaken the economies of the developed countries and destroy those of the undeveloped nations.

These problems are compounded by 'an energy crisis that has intensified inflationary trends and balance-of-payments deficits in the industrialized countries and is enriching the coffers of nations whose underdeveloped economies are as yet unable to absorb large amounts of capital; and by an international monetary crisis in which money manipulators could conceivably undermine the currencies of the highly industrialized nations.

Help for the Have-Nots

No nation can prosper indefinitely if two-thirds of the world's nations are in need. Charity does not begin only at home, for charity abroad may forestall trouble at home. Foreign aid is not charity, but insurance against global chaos.

Nevertheless, as Mr. Lewis points out, for years our foreign policy was so hopelessly entangled in the morass of Vietnam that our policy-makers could not deal with the world economic situation. "Over-population and mass starvation are just around the corner, and they are going to happen in our lifetime. Millions and probably hundreds of millions of people in this world are going to starve to death. It's a grim fact to face, but it's true."

Another crisis requiring immediate attention is that of resources. The industrialized nations are becoming more dependent economically on the producers of raw materials. The United States, for example, is no longer self-sufficient in the production of copper or bauxite, while Japan and some of the nations of Western Europe are completely dependent for oil on outside sources.

While the industrial and agricultural powers increase production to meet their ever-growing needs, the poorer nations of the world slip more deeply into poverty. With their populations growing at an uncontrolled rate, any gains they make in productivity are offset by the population increase. Nor can they afford to import the food that they need, or the fertilizer and the equipment that would aid them in increasing food production, or the technology that they need to develop their own industries, for the costs of food, energy, fertilizers, and industrial products have risen astronomically.

Dr. Fatemi warned the "have" nations: "If the fact that two-thirds of the world's population lives at subsistence level does not disturb the conscience of the wealthier third of the world, it should prompt the people of the developed nations to consider that this problem will sooner or later affect them. For poverty breeds disease, instability, ignorance, hatred, and violence.

"In 1946 the rest of the world had no money, so that we had to give away billions of dollars. Today, much of the world has financial resources—not only the oil-producing countries, the copper-producing countries, but many other nations as well. There are rising expectations all over the world. Other countries need more food; they need technology. The question now is whether or not we have a plan for the next ten years to help them, not as a superior power, but as a partner. If we sell to them, buy from them, and give them our technology without conditions, then I think we. ourselves, will profit more than any other country."

Finally, there is the problem of pollution. The more the nations of the world develop industry, the more they poison the world's oceans, waterways, and atmosphere. There can be no national solutions to the problem of pollution, for the oceans and the atmosphere span the globe. The industrial wastes that one nation pours into them sooner or later pollute the air and water of others—further evidence of interdependence.

A First Summation

The conclusions reached by the panelists about the problems facing the United States can be summarized as follows: Physically, we live in a single world, made smaller by advances in technology, in transportation, and in communications; yet this same world is very much divided economically, ideologically, and psychologically. At a time when cooperation among nations is necessary to solve such large-scale problems, competition—economic, ideological, political, and military—obscures the real issues and makes their solution impossible.

Alleviation of economic problems is a major key to the relief of many of the world's ills, but the conflict among nations is consuming the money, energy, and resources needed for social and economic betterment. If the nations of the world—the producers of raw materials and the consumers, the industrialized and nonindustrialized, the rich and poor, communist and non-communist, black and white, brown and yellow—do not work together to limit conflict and overcome the problems that plague all, then surely we shall all hang together.

*   *   *   *

Despite efforts at détente and displays of friendship and in spite of any treaties or agreements, Washington's future course must take full account of the other two of the "Big Three." At one of the panels, intimate views of the two communist giants were presented. These profiles are summarized in the next chapter.

Chapter 3
COMMUNIST MYSTERIES

Russia and China, the two communist giants, will surely loom large in our future. Both are lands of mystery, and we negotiate with them in a kind of diplomatic fog. What sort of people are these? What sort of lives do they lead? Here are reports from correspondents who have spent long periods in the two capitals or made special studies of developments there.

Mr. Grose provided an overall impression of life in Soviet society:

"After two years of living in the Soviet Union, I am reminded first of the suppression of individuality. The great individual feeling for which the Russian people have been notorious and which has been celebrated in literature and art for centuries apparently no longer exists. The leaders and philosophers of the regime have made a virtue of suppressing what we call individuality and have replaced it with what they label a greater good: Collective virtue is

40

far preferable to individual virtue and the whole is greater than the sum of its parts. That sounds harsh, and I mean it to sound harsh. I think the basic factor in the system of Communist Party rule, as it has developed in the Soviet Union, is that the collective counts for everything, while the individual counts for distressingly little.

"Most of the people accept this condition gladly. Let's not delude ourselves. There's no popular unrest. Indeed, for the vast majority of the Soviet people, living today is far more comfortable, far more attractive, far more satisfying than anything their grandparents could have hoped for. But I don't think individuals of sensitivity and intelligence as, Lord knows, the Russian people are, can accept suppression of their individuality for very long."

Mr. Salisbury was asked about the reasons for the dissidence in Russian society. He described the tremendous political and economic problems facing the Soviet government and added: "I would spell out their situation in terms like this. They're fifty-five years into a revolution, which is now very old and tired. They have lost sight of the idealistic objectives which were to create a better order and a more equitable relationship between human beings, to bring an end to suffering, want, and oppression, to create heaven on earth. This was the dream in the minds of Lenin and all those young idealists who fought for a hundred years to bring revolution to Russia.

"Now after fifty-five years, what confronts the Russian people? They're faced with a leadership of gray, old, tired, sagging bureaucrats, all of them products of the most stultifying kind of routine imaginable. They are little men, fearful of being displaced, afraid of their own countrymen. They are men who have been trained not to have ideas, because ideas are extremely dangerous. And what is the result? They have a sagging economy that has lost the vitality it had when Russia entered the industrial revolution back in the thirties. Now their economic rate of growth and expansion slips a little bit every year. They simply can't expand with the methods they have and with a bureaucracy that is strangling them.

"As for their agriculture, before the revolution, Russia was a great food-exporting nation; after 1917 she never has been. The communists have never been able to cope with agriculture; their failures brought them face to face with famine only the summer before last."

Is the Soviet economic situation then so bleak that the communist state has been weakened? Mr. Kleiman offered a picture quite different from Mr. Salisbury's:

A Nation of Power

"The ideals of the communists are very high-sounding, and some of them have been realized. They have industrialized not only manufacturing but also agriculture. Their gross national product has grown at an extraordinary rate. Even if Soviet statistics are challenged to a certain extent, they have had a faster growth rate until recent years than most of the developed world, but that is partly because the Soviet Union was an underdeveloped country. Nevertheless, there have been great successes.

"The communists have created a military power equivalent to that of the United States and they have absorbed neighboring territories so they now have a great nation of mounting world power controlled at the top of a pyramid by a small group determined to improve the lot of their people and to invest heavily in further industrialization.

"The consumer sector has always had shortages, and if

you visit a department store in Moscow you find many things that people don't want to buy; the items people do want have long since disappeared. There are lots of electric razors, plenty of television sets and radios, but shoddy clothing at very high prices. You remember the story about the movie of American workers being beaten up by the police in Chicago and the Soviet audience watching this horrible scene shouting, 'Look at those shoes!'

"But things are changing. There's tremendous housing construction in Moscow. You rarely find, as when I first went there in 1947, six or seven families living in a railroad flat, one family per room. Almost every family in Moscow has its own apartment now. They're small and shabby but they have a certain degree of privacy which they never had before. The standard of living has increased, but at the same time one senses a great drabness in Russian life."

If the majority are content, then why is such rigid control necessary? Why are free speech and a free press forbidden? This was Mr. Kleiman's explanation: "Russia has been autocratic traditionally and has never known freedom in our sense. After a very brief interlude of democratic rule, the czars were succeeded by the Bolsheviks, who do not believe in a democratic society as we understand it, but in a dictatorship of the proletariat, which actually means rule by the communist party, which proclaims itself the spokesman, representative, and intellect of the proletariat. The Party has developed a military police state in order to establish a self-perpetuating oligarchy and maintain its unchallenged authority. And so you have a kind of communist corporate state in which the corporate leaders employ all the power of the state against any dissident voices."

The Internal Impact

Mr. Kleiman was asked if the growing sophistication of Soviet society could be expected to encourage the importation of Western ideas. He replied:

"The Voice of America is no longer being jammed, nor the BBC, nor the German or French radios. The Russians can and do listen very widely, and they compare the news from the foreign radio with what appears in the Soviet press. The Soviet media have to respond to information that they have never reported, because the Soviet population has heard it on foreign broadcasts. And so there is now an opening in Soviet society which is extraordinary when compared to anything that existed in the past; and yet curiously enough, despite this, Russia remains very much a closed society under close control.

"There is no tradition of democracy and freedom in the Soviet Union, and there is a tendency on the part of the bulk of the population to believe what it is told, to follow the leaders. They are in a period of evolution, but I think it will be a very long time before there is any substantial development of freedom unless there is a breakdown in the structure, which I don't anticipate, or a defeat in a war, which I don't see happening. However, there now exists a certain amount of dissidence in Soviet society in addition to that which is well-known, such as that of Solzhenitsyn and Sakharov. There is a much higher degree of education today than in the past. People attend universities and the higher schools in such large numbers that a certain amount of questioning is certain to develop.

"This does not mean that a Western type of liberalization of democracy is evolving, but only that there is a beginning of questioning within the Soviet structure and the development of groups which may have an interest in relations with the outside world."

From Inside China

The talk then turned to the other communist giant, China. Mrs. Topping was asked what was the outstanding single impression, the first picture of that country that came to her mind:

"My very first impression is one of a nation that's developing at a fast pace; a country that in 1949 was down at the heels and had nowhere to go but up. After the communists took over things began to happen.

"I lived in Nanking for two years while the Revolution was going on, and I left when the communists came into the city. When I returned for the first time eighteen years later, in 1966, I barely recognized the city, or China. The country had been cleaned up, morally and physically, but the thing that impressed me most was the change in the people's attitude, from a negative to a positive one. They're laboring for the collective, and for the state, but in that sense they're working for themselves, because without a country, without a state, what do you have? You have nothing if you don't have your country.

"At the time of the Revolution, China was on the brink of collapse. This government has unified the country, brought the people together and given them a common cause, and now they're working together for the betterment of China itself and for greater stature in the world. If we can say one thing about China, it is that in the last twenty-four years it has become a nation that is recognized as an equal by the world community."

What, then, was the need for the Cultural Revolution,

if conditions are so good? Mrs. Topping replied: "The purpose of the Cultural Revolution is to keep the society in flux. The dialectical materialists said years ago that in a revolutionary society things must be kept moving and developing. As China arrives at one level, contradictions arise, so they have to advance to another level. Every eight years, as Mao Tse-tung says, there is to be a cultural revolution. The Chinese never said the Cultural Revolution was over. They said the first stage, the violent stage, had been completed. But the Revolution will continue as long as this present regime lasts in China. It's part of it."

Asked to make a comparison between individual freedom under Chiang Kai-shek and under Mao Tse-tung, Mrs. Topping said: "Of course, the Chinese are paying a price for their improvements. The cost is individual freedom. But I know a lot of old ladies in New York who would pay the price of personal liberty to have the freedom to walk through a crime-free street. The Chinese have paid a price, but they have gained something too.

"There's one other thing we have to take into account when we automatically assume that our type of democracy would be good for the Soviet Union or good for China. How could a country with over 800 million people function under the type of democracy that we have? It would be absolute chaos; after all, it's pretty chaotic here."

The Red Giants Compared

Mrs. Topping was then asked what are the important differences between China and Russia—ideology, territory, race, economy?

"The divergence between the two countries lies in a combination of all these things, but I think probably the greatest differences are in tradition and race. The ideological contrast results from differences in these other areas and also from the national characteristics of the Chinese people. The basic Marxist-Leninist theory that was adopted by the Soviet Communists is the same as that adopted by the Chinese, but Maoist philosophy has made an additional distinction. Maoist doctrine, in a way, imposes the traditional, national characteristics, the character of China itself, upon communism. It's hard for me to say what one factor is the most significant, but I would think that because they are so close territorially their fear of each other's intentions is a very important element.

Mrs. Topping, asked if she had been surprised by the recent attack on the formerly venerated Confucius, answered: "Not necessarily. For whom was he writing? Confucius wrote for the male elite of the old society. He was a male chauvinist pig, as a matter of fact. I'm not surprised when they take a man like Confucius, who wrote only for a certain limited class of society, and attack him now as an example of a false leader. Now they want to break that old society down; they want to bring people onto an equal level, so they attack Confucius."

As for the social pattern in China—the crime rate, the suicide rate, poverty, and government suppression of ideas —Mrs. Topping said: "I have no idea of the crime rate because, as in the Soviet Union, there are no statistics published. But China has managed to eliminate organized crime so that we know the crime rate is much lower than in the United States. They've broken the drug rings and there are no narcotics in China today, except for medicinal uses.

"As you know, opium was one of the biggest problems of China in 1949. Shortly after the communists came in they rounded up the drug addicts and pushers. They executed the pushers, but not those who sold drugs because of their addiction. They put all addicts into rehabilitation centers. The leaders said to the people of China that drug addicts were not to be persecuted by society, because they were victims of the old system. It was the responsibility of members of the new society to rehabilitate them and make them useful citizens. I think one can honestly say there is no longer any drug addiction there.

"As far as crime is concerned, there is no organized crime in China. There are no longer any organized prostitution rings or gambling rings, nor any graft. There are no store owners, but those that manage the stores don't have to pay anybody for protection any more, as in the old days of the terror rings."

How Much We Know

These observations about the two communist nations led finally to the question of how much we know about them. Professor Hollander commented: "We know much less about China than we do about the Soviet Union for a number of reasons, one being that until recently the Chinese permitted very few foreign visitors. Even today the foreign visitors who are being allowed into China are fairly carefully selected, and movement is rather limited, much more so than in the Soviet Union. Also, very few outsiders know Chinese.

"The Soviet Union has become a more open society than China (and I am by no means an admirer of the Soviet Union, my departure from Hungary in 1956 after the revolution not having predisposed me to veneration of the USSR). Many more visitors go to Russia; there are more exchange programs with Western universities; the Russians are publishing much more that interests Westerners: social science studies, historical treatises, personal recollections. So in my opinion there is absolutely no comparison between how much we know about the Soviet Union and how much we know about China.

"The partial opening-up of China is very recent. I have read not only many current travel accounts of China, but I have also talked to a number of people who have visited the country. There are severe restrictions on what foreigners can see there; whereas people who go to the Soviet Union today can see a great deal more, even though probably two-thirds to three-fourths of the Soviet Union is off limits to foreign visitors.

"Also, there is another very obvious problem which people who have visited China pointed out to me. A Westerner just can't get lost in the crowd in China, unless he is an overseas Chinese who is back on a visit, whereas in the Soviet Union foreigners are somewhat less conspicuous. There is also an element of informal social control at work in China. Visitors report that even though they are allowed to wander about, crowds gather around them immediately so the likelihood of too many spontaneous exchanges between foreigners, even those who know Chinese, and the natives, is very limited."

Mrs. Topping disagreed with Dr. Hollander's statement that Russia has a much more open society than China: "During the three years I spent in the Soviet Union as a writer and photographer I found much more repression than when I worked in China. In Russia I was given a list of things that I could not photograph. In China we could take photographs freely of anything we saw, with only two exceptions: some submarines in the Yangtze River in Shanghai Harbor and the subway in Peking, because it housed air-raid shelters."

Did Mrs. Topping feel that freedom of information existed in China? "I'm not saying that China has an open society by any means. But I don't think it's any more closed a society than that of the Soviet Union. It's true that a foreigner can't get lost in China, but he's not followed around as he might be in the Soviet Union. One can talk to the Chinese if he speaks the language."

But whether Russia is more open than China or vice versa is a futile debate because the fact is that both are nations in which the reporter is restricted both as to what he sees and what he hears. So again it should be said that to negotiate with the communists is to play poker in a fog.

*   *   *   *

This is the kind of report the reader gets from the correspondent when he is free to talk and to write free of supervision or censorship. That raises the question of the news that moves into and out of countries. How accurate, how responsible, how understandable is the flow of the news? The issue—one of prime importance in surveying the international landscape—is discussed in the next chapter.

Chapter 4
FLOW OF THE NEWS

The flow of the news among nations is a major factor in international affairs for two reasons: first, because it is an important element in creating the images nations have of one another and, second, because there is always the danger that it will be used for propaganda purposes.

The problem was studied by the researchers and dissected by a panel consisting of four Americans who reported on the image of the U.S. abroad, and four foreign correspondents who reported on the coverage of their countries in the American press.

In general the impression was that the flow was faulty; that, with few exceptions, it consisted of trivial or sensational instead of substantial news; that it failed to provide interpretation; and that it tended to build inaccurate pictures of the outside world.

The indictment was first put to the news service people, who supply more than 90% of the foreign news that appears in the press in the U.S. and the rest of the world. The wire service men held—not surprisingly—that the flow of international news is essentially good. But from various studies, including our own, we had concluded that it is faulty. We asked for comments on our conclusions.

Mr. Swinton of the Associated Press agreed that the point that there was too much trivia was well taken. "There certainly is a lot of minutia that goes over the wires. And that's natural. People are interested in the sex life of Hollywood stars and starlets, or of Italian stars and starlets."

Is the foreign news covered by the media understandable, that is, does it include sufficient background and explanation? Mr. Swinton said that there is now more interpretation going over the wires, "and that's a good thing." Wilbur Landry, Foreign Editor of the United Press International, was not so sure that more interpretation was an unmitigated advantage; straight news was perhaps more desirable because "when a story goes over the wires and it's important, over one billion people see it. Now that is a hell of a responsibility."

Interpretation, it had been said, was the first thing killed by editors when newspaper space is needed. Mr. Swinton commented: "Not quite. If you send out a news interpretation piece a day or two ahead, then they set it in type and it makes it. If you move it the same day, it gets pushed out. There is more interpretation, and hopefully it's improved over the years."

Is Our Press Provincial?

Mr. Middleton felt that American newspapers and news services tend to be provincial, but that parochialism in the

United States is more understandable than it is in Britain or France: "After all, if you're in Omaha, you're a lot farther from Chicago than you are from Paris if you're in London."

Mr. Nagata said that American newspapers tend to be more provincial than those of Japan. "The big difference between the American press structure and that of Japan is that in Japan the newspapers are large, nationwide dailies which have a national circulation and provide good space to international reporting. If you go into the countryside in Japan you can still get the international news. As I understand it, in the United States there are the very distinguished papers like the *New York Times* and the *Washington Post,* but there are many local papers which do not carry much international news. The only nationwide source is television."

Mr. von Krusenstiern said that although the major American media—television, the news weeklies, and the major newspapers—are doing very well, "there is fairly thorough coverage only on the East coast and probably on one-and-a-half spots on the West coast; in between you have very little, except television, which is basically doing a good job, but cannot do it sufficiently. Also, in between, you have the news weeklies, which are one medium I consider constantly underrated. The news magazines are filling the gap left by the newspapers between the East and West coasts."

Mr. Shishkin observed that "such newspapers as the *New York Times,* the *Washington Post,* the *Christian Science Monitor,* the *Baltimore Sun,* and maybe the *Los Angeles Times* do devote attention to the Soviet Union, but if you read the provincial press you will notice that its reports about the Soviet Union are very scanty; there is a local ignorance outside of big metropolitan centers about the Soviet Union. The same can be said about American television. It is very important," Mr. Shishkin concluded, "that the American media report more about my country."

Causes of Distortion

The next question dealt with the image issue. Is American press coverage of foreign countries distorted?

Mr. Nagata said that images of other countries may be distorted simply because good coverage is not easy: "First, I think it is very difficult for foreigners to get good overall pictures of other countries. About ten years ago I met somebody who worked in this country. He told me that if one stays three days in Moscow, he can write an article; if he stays three weeks, perhaps he will write a book; but if he stays more than three years then he may possibly not write anything. Second, even though a foreign correspondent tries to cover a country as accurately as possible, he can misunderstand, be prejudiced, or lack knowledge, and he may therefore distort the images of other countries."

Mr. Shishkin said that he felt American press coverage is still biased because of a lack of perspective. "It still concentrates on and exaggerates single episodes in Soviet life out of proportion to the rest and thus creates false images. For example, the problem of so-called Soviet dissidents, especially Solzhenitsyn, is overplayed in the American press, while other, more important problems are sacrificed. There is a tendency which is even worse, I think, to present the Soviet Union in the role of a man begging for favors from the United States with cup in hand. This I would call a very false image of the Soviet Union."

Several correspondents said that editorial decisions can often distort news that is supplied by reporters in the field. David Webster said that although a correspondent may have a balanced idea of life in the country to which he is assigned, "he will find his reports constantly distorted by somebody back at his base, whose notions suffer from a cultural lag and a set of assumptions picked up in other media. It takes a good, tough, hard correspondent of some seniority to tell the person at base to get lost, that he is not interested in covering a particular story. My argument is that editorial power should as far as possible be given to the people in the field."

Mr. Swinton also stressed the importance of editors in the transmission of news: "The copy editor is the person who actually puts the news in the paper, and sometimes the decision about who becomes a copy editor is a strange one. I think perhaps we're addressing ourselves to things like the flow of the news without getting down to the gut issue of who puts the news in the paper."

Mr. von Krusenstiern observed that "national images tend to be one or even two generations out of date. The reason for this is pretty simple. Even in the affluent countries, only a fairly small percentage of people have the chance to travel abroad, to become acquainted with other countries. The image most people have of other countries is formed by parents and by teachers, and that is one generation apart."

Mr. Webster pointed out that when one attempts to communicate facts about another country, one must also deal with the assumptions of those who receive the facts: "The picture of Britain in the United States," he observed, "is complicated by the fact that most people here already think they know about Britain."

Thus the foreign editors indicated that the flow might well be more solid and more accurate. Then the procedure was reversed, and the American correspondents were asked to evaluate the images of the United States as reported in the media of other countries.

The American Views

Mr. Middleton felt that none of the images of the United States is even approximately accurate, although "I would say that the BBC, the *London Times,* the *Economist,* and the *Telegraph* provide pretty good pictures."

Is there no more understanding of the United States abroad today than there was at the end of World War II? Mr. Middleton said that the level of understanding is far higher than it used to be. "Yes, there are the stereotypes— the American tourist with his cameras and Hawaiian shirt —but I think other people know a good deal more about America now than they did, and it isn't just because of the tourists; it's because of the American news agencies and the American newspapers that circulate in Europe."

Mr. Landrey observed that when he was a correspondent in London in the fifties and sixties "the United States was sort of an amiable, somewhat dimwitted and naive cousin who happened to strike it rich. The stories in those days tended to be, at least in one segment of the press, about swallowing goldfish and about panty raids. I am told that the situation hasn't changed in that respect—that streaking still gets quite a good press. But our reporters say that they discern a more serious attempt to understand the United States on the part of the major media. Even in France."

Then there are the problems that affect the transmission of news about the United States to other countries.

Mr. von Krusenstiern reported that what the American wire services provide is always filtered through local nationals and that it is local people who "translate the report into the local language, or the local wire service handles it in bulk. Or sometimes they transmit it in English to the local newspapers, and then the strangest things can happen. I remember about ten years ago I was responsible for the German-language service of UPI. I came in one morning and read the overnight German-language report. There was a strange story about something which had happened to an old man from the California community of Ucla. You develop a sense for this kind of thing, so I checked the original story in English and discovered that the person involved had been a senior from U.C.L.A."

Mr. Webster mentioned the parochialism of the British press: "I am greatly disturbed that most British journals look like one of those fabled small newspapers of the American Middle West. Journalism in Britain is essentially parochial. The great British public does not seem to care a damn about Cyprus or Aden or India, or anywhere else in the world since their relationship to these countries has been greatly diminished. You will always find that the local fire will take precedence over a major cataclysm wherever it may be, unless that cataclysm puts British mothers' sons in peril. And this is one of the factors in British journalism, both broadcast and print, which worries people like me, because in our news reporting we are very much more parochial than the major organs of American journalism."

The correspondents had listed translation difficulties, distortion by copy editors, and lack of concern over significant news about other countries as problems affecting the transmission of news about the United States.

A Mutual Distrust

Mr. Shishkin brought up the problem of the mutual suspicion that exists between the United States and the Soviet Union as a factor affecting the exchange of news. He observed, though, that "these two very important nations are entering into a new epoch, a new stage of development, a period of transition from confrontation to negotiation and cooperation. This transitional period can't be easy. There is the inheritance of mutual suspicion, or mutual distrust, which originated with the October Revolution and multiplied during what you call the Cold War. From this point of view, I support Mr. Markel's conviction that it is a prime task of the news media to contribute to the removal of this distrust, to contribute to mutual understanding between people."

Problems of mutual suspicion and distrust apply, of course, particularly to Russia and China. Until the iron and bamboo curtains are removed, these doubts will remain. Mr. Kleiman spoke of the difficulties in Russia. He admitted that there is a very complicated psychological problem involved: "When you get to know a Russian, you're always wondering whether you're exposing him to danger because of his contacts with a foreigner, and if you're not exposing him to danger, whether he's reporting regularly to the secret police. This makes contact between foreigners and Russians extremely difficult. The present leaders are much more cautious and not as visible as Khrushchev was. But we do have access now to a much larger and wider variety of Soviet intellectuals."

Mr. Grose agreed that a reporter has a problem with access to places and people in the Soviet Union; however, he said: "There is a sharp distinction in the minds of Russian citizens between casual encounters—I've had many interesting discussions standing in a subway train in Moscow or in a Moscow café where they didn't know my name—and formal encounters, in which there is an implied commitment of seeing each other again; then the situation becomes delicate. So a major problem is simply access to what people are thinking."

Mr. Grose felt that the American correspondent could get a good deal of information from the Soviet press. He said, "I'll never forget when I first went to Moscow that one of the *New York Times* editors kept saying to me, 'Don't keep quoting *Pravda*. We're sick and tired of stories that quote *Pravda* and *Komsomolskaya Pravda*. Quote people, don't quote newspapers.' He looked upon a statement in one of the papers as one would have considered a White House pronouncement. As a matter of fact, a statement published in *Pravda* is even more official than a statement made by Ron Ziegler in Washington would have been, because the *Pravda* statement is a carefully thought-out presentation of the official point of view."

Are Russian newspapers, then, a source of accurate information about the Soviet Union?

"One thing," said Mr. Grose, "which people in this country seldom realize is that Russians are informed of things by reading *Pravda,* not necessarily about the realities of the world around them, but about political issues. And so citing a point out of *Pravda* is not lazy reporting or simply picking up the local press; this is reporting the political viewpoint of the ruling circles. At some points in the Soviet political evolution you could learn a lot by simply comparing the political commentaries of the newspaper which represents the Party view and the newspaper which represents the government view. There is a lot that one can learn by a careful analysis of what is written in the Soviet press."

Then one recalls that a free press and free speech do not exist in Russia, and the suspicion is revived. The communist current is a powerful one in the flow of the news and until its waters move freely there will be mistrust.

PART II:
THE "IDEAL LEADER"

In Part I there was presented the background of the basic decision the United States must make about its role in the world. Now these questions arise: What role does national leadership play in determining the new role? How well-equipped are our leaders, the President and the Congress, for the task? Who have been the great Presidents? What are the qualities they have brought to the office? These questions are discussed in the following chapters.

Chapter 5
COMMANDER-IN-CHIEF

The prime functions of the Presidential office are communication, enlightenment, inspiration—the establishment of understanding with the people, a constant effort to inform and educate them. Above all, the President must have credibility. Take the office as it is today. As a result of false information about Vietnam and Cambodia, unwarranted claims of victory, and especially the tissue of lies woven around Watergate, Mr. Ford inherited a large burden of distrust. In his relations with the people his primary task is to reestablish faith in his words.

His is a lonely post. "The President," says Tom Wicker, "is probably more isolated today than any comparable political officer has been since the days of absolute monarchy. He has been forced to rely more and more on staff reports by 'experts' and other secondhand sources. The problem is compounded by the inevitable workings of bureaucracy, the tendency of staff men to become yes men."

The consequence of this isolation is pointed out by Mr. Reedy: "One of the most important tasks for a President is somehow or other to maintain a sense of objectivity about himself, to fight off the disease of self-centered thought, which is very virulent in the White House. It is there, even though it may not be so poisonous as it was in the case of the ex-Nazi schoolmaster, Heinrich Himmler, who wanted to establish an academy of astral physics to prove his own conclusion that stars are made of ice.

"The inclination to seek only what you want to find, and to find only what you are looking for, to confirm your prejudices, is very, very strong in the case of the Presidency. The problem though is how do you institute within the Presidency the kind of adversary proceeding that is needed? There is the Senate but it is not a bureaucracy, rather a group of free-floating feudal barons, each secure in his base.

"Moreover, when you institutionalize the adversary, you can say: Okay, now I've listened to him; let's forget him. This kind of thing happened in the Vietnam debate when George Ball, Under-Secretary of State, was the institutionalized adversary. Once he had said his piece, the President felt that he had been objective, having listened to all sides, and went ahead and did exactly what he wanted to do anyway."

The President must fight the tendency to accept favorable information and reject unfavorable. He must meet regularly with representatives of the various groups and divisions in the country, Democrats and Republicans, spokesmen for the East as well as the West, representatives of the minority as well as representatives of the majority.

Mr. Truman said, "The President must communicate with the people to avoid the risk of a loss of public confidence."

A Vague, Unique Job

As for the range of the Presidential assignment, Mr. Reedy feels that its dimensions cannot be measured "except possibly by someone who has studied Aristotelian metaphysics and probed the question of infinity. The job in and of itself is a unique one, simply because the Constitution—quite wisely, I think—says very little about it and sets up very few barriers around it. About all the Constitution really says is that all executive powers shall be invested in the President.

"The Founding Fathers did not use the type of reasoning that became so popular later: to set down ground rules, to footnote, and to amend. To check political ambitions, they did not define Presidential power in such a way as to harness men and so thwart the greedy, but rather set up competing institutions to maintain some sort of balance.

"When one tries to define the job of the Presidency in terms of its outer limits, one is very quickly lost, because history makes it apparent that today's outer limits will be far exceeded in tomorrow's Presidency and then exceeded in turn. When we elect a man, we give him a hunting license and, with fervent hope, tell him: 'Go forth and do good.'

"What a President does is limited only by his imagination and by the strength of the competing institutions—the Congress, the courts and, strangely enough, the informal checks that run through our society, such as the federal/state system, the limits on the economic resources upon which he can draw, his need to maintain himself with some degree of prudence in order to hold the country together.

"The question, however, can be approached in another way. It is customary to start out by listing all the various things a President is: political leader, legislative initiator, moral spokesman, voice in foreign affairs, manipulator; the list is endless because what the President really is, is the ultimate in executive power. The well-known sign that Mr. Truman had over his desk—'The Buck Stops Here'—is really a very good definition of the Presidency; the boundaries cannot be delineated more clearly than that.

"But there are two Presidential roles which can be defined and which provide clues to the nature of the job: First, he is the man who sustains the unity of the nation; he is the symbol of that unity; and the only mechanism through which that unity can be expressed. Second, he is the leader of the nation, the director of its affairs, the manager of its business, for his four-year term.

"In diplomatic parlance the first role is usually known as that of 'chief of state'; the second as that of 'chief of government'. Most Americans, because we are so accustomed to our form of government, are totally unaware that only in the Western hemisphere, and one or two isolated spots such as the Philippines, are both roles lodged in one man.

Clash of the Two Roles

"The two roles are fundamentally incompatible, an incompatibility that has led to a major problem. Even though the President is presumed to be above the struggle, he is nevertheless the national leader; and leadership by very definition is a political question. What we have done, without intending to do it, is to create an office which has built into it a form of schizophrenia—on the one hand, there is a man who is accorded full reverence—a status from which nothing can add or detract except death or revolution; on the other hand, a man who is engaged in the hard, sweaty tasks of leadership. Thus the two roles clash; the role of unifier is tarnished by the political leadership role. And, the role of leader requires a kind of intuitive perception—a feeling for other people that can come only through involvement in the struggles of daily life. So we are asking a man to withdraw from the political forces that sweep the nation and at the same time to plunge right into them.

"The result of the clash has been a series of very unsatisfactory Presidents and as the nation becomes more complex and the leaders lose direct contact with the people, we are going to find it more and more difficult to discover the kind of leaders we need.

"Consider what is involved in the role of chief of state, of being the unifying factor in the nation. Mr. Nixon, like Lyndon Johnson, was fond of referring to himself as 'President of all the people.' The phrase is not merely a rhetorical flourish; it reveals a deep-seated truth about our government, which is that we really have only one President at a time—the sole spokesman for the nation, no matter how reluctant many people may be to accept him in the role.

"Now if you are to select the ideal man for this role, obviously you would choose one who really did speak for all of the people or at least a majority of them. This is impractical, unless you go to some sort of constitutional monarchy in which the monarch is set above political struggle. Then you really would have a man who could unify the nation while its affairs were being carried on by others.

But in the United States this is impossible because we have lodged in the one man both the unifying and managerial roles."

"Ike" the Adroit

Mr. Reedy then cited the unique case of General Eisenhower: "I can think of only one modern President that was capable, for a long period of time, of sustaining the sort of posture required of a sacred emblem of unity— Dwight D. Eisenhower. At the time, partisan Democrats like me and, for that matter, quite a few Republicans thought of him as a do-nothing type, sort of dumb and happy. Since then I have changed my view somewhat, because the eight Eisenhower years were the only eight in modern times when we had a relative amount of serenity and a relative amount of unity. And when the President left office his standing was about the same as when he entered.

"I say this even though I think we paid a rather heavy price for those eight years; the management of our affairs during that period was poor and many of the problems we face today arose out of the inaction that marked the Eisenhower terms.

"Eisenhower really did try to play the role of the presiding monarch, leaving, as much as he could, the tasks of management to others who were engaged in the hard, everyday tasks of existence.

"On the whole we had unity and there was a great deal of approval of the Eisenhower way. But we had, at the same time, a type of government which was not aggressive or forceful and which did not tackle many current problems. I am convinced that earlier and more energetic action on the question of civil rights—vigorous enforcement of what flowed from the Supreme Court decision of 1954—would have left us in a far stronger position than that today. I think we paid heavily for the temporizing."

Mr. Hyman added this footnote: "One of the things that would be important to remember about General Eisenhower was that he brought his own legend with him. He said a supreme commander can never appear wrong. Field commanders, however, can appear wrong—they are expendable and you can sack them. And he applied that attitude to his cabinet; these were his field commanders, while he, as President, was the supreme commander.

"Eisenhower was extremely adroit in using his cabinet officers to deflect attack from himself. Also it should be remembered that he was the only American in modern times who came to the Presidency with his place in history secure. He could not go any higher; the only way he could go was down. He was very jealous of his reputation."

Three Presidential Types

Mr. Hyman then analyzed the Presidential types: "In the past," he said, "it was possible to choose a President from about three kinds of models—Buchanan Presidencies, Lincolnian Presidencies, and Cleveland Presidencies. All three were constitutional but they did represent different types—giving the impression, from an analytical standpoint, of different kinds of *geist*.

"The Buchanan type was legalistic in emphasis. It conceived of the work of the Presidency as being performed within a tight legal circuit involving the Congress and the Supreme Court. The President merely administered the objectives and situations turned over to him by the Congress; he did not feel it was his duty to fight for the things he considered desirable. His aim was to bring dignity and decorum to the conduct of government and to ensure efficiency and economy in the civil service. Above all, a Buchanan President felt he was doing a fine job if he got along with the Congress.

"The Buchanan Presidents did not want to disturb things; they looked upon the past as a great golden age in which all men were demi-gods and all women woodland nymphs.

"Whether this philosophy was congruous with the actual needs of the hour was another matter. But it was a constitutional type of Presidency and, in retrospect, you could recognize that the Buchanan Presidency coincided with the ascendancy in the nation of the first of what I would call three psychological parties: the party of memory; the party of hope; and the limitist party.

The Lincoln Method

"The Lincolnian type of Presidency was at the opposite end; it was essentially political as against legalistic in emphasis. Whereas a Buchanan Presidency put its gravitational center in the Presidential office—a hard, plastic, Apollonian kind of thing governed by laws—a Lincolnian Presidency put its gravitational center in the institution, a kind of a Dionysian place, full of music, dreams, hopes, boundless expectation.

"In a Lincolnian Presidency the President was placed neither above the Congress nor below it, neither above the Court nor below it. He felt he had a mandate of his own, that what were needed were a strong Congress, a strong Court, and a strong Presidency. He was always subject to charges that he was spendthrift and bent on usurpation of power. Nonetheless, he aimed to bring the country a rekindling of hope, a reshuffling of the wheel of fortune, and a redress of grievances long endured. And just as a Buchanan Presidency tended to appear on the scene when the party of memory was in the ascendancy, a Lincolnian type of Presidency tended to appear when the party of hope was on the rise.

"In between the concept of the Buchanan Presidency and the Lincolnian Presidency, there was the Cleveland Presidency. It was a hybrid Presidency that shifted from the Apollonian view to the Dionysian institution; now it spoke of marching forward to new horizons and now it took a backward step for every one forward. Now it gave the Congress its head; now it stopped the Congress in its tracks.

"If there was any distinctive aspect to the Cleveland Presidency, it was that its strength lay essentially in the veto power. It did not initiate things; it stopped things, appearing to be content to maintain a kind of kinetic equilibrium, like a motor idling but going nowhere. And the Cleveland Presidency tended to coincide with the ascendancy in the nation of the limitist party.

A Changing Office

"If there were these three fairly clear types of presidencies in times past, today the three lines have become as indistinct as lines drawn in water. One reason may be the fact that the program and the philosophies of the parties have become almost indistinguishable. At times we are nostalgic for the past, at other times we are hopeful for the future, thinking that if this or this happens we may march at least to the suburbs of Utopia and, with some luck, maybe into the main city. There was always this mixture of cross tensions and cross moves, but now it seems to me, the confusion, the Babel, the confusion of tongues is so great that it represents something entirely new."

But whether or not the Presidency is entering a new phase, what is certain is that in this tangled world it is an office of constantly increasing complexities and difficulties, as Mr. Hyman pointed out:

"One reason why the Presidency now differs so greatly from those of earlier days is that the question of whom the President represents has new aspects. More than ever before a President has two constituencies: a domestic voting constituency from which he derives his title of office and a nonvoting foreign constituency that is affected by everything he does. He is caught between these two constituencies; in his response to the domestic constituency, he may act like a Buchanan President, or a Lincoln President, or he may act entirely differently with respect to his external constituency when foreign affairs are involved.

"Once these things happened one at a time and the President could think solely in terms of domestic affairs or solely in terms of foreign affairs. Now he must think simultaneously of both.

"Another element of confusion arises because so many of our political views these days are entwined with scientific and technological questions. Before you can come to a good judgment on the political side of an issue, you have to extract from it a scientific and technological base.

"Because of this, the old constitutional positions are no longer relevant; what is relevant is exact knowledge. You no longer argue in legalistic terms; you either know or don't know what are the technological aspects of a political issue. Decisions become much more complicated and difficult. For example, the President may turn for advice on a political-scientific issue to three Nobel prize winners, one in physics, one in chemistry, and a third in biology, and the three may disagree with one another. How is the President, an amateur, to decide which is the expert to whom he should listen?"

Information: A Moot Issue

These statements led naturally to questions about the information a President receives and his selection and use of advisers. Mr. Reedy was reassuring on that score:

"A considerable amount of effort has been misdirected in attempting to find ways of making sure that Presidents shall have the facts needed for decision-making. The truth is—based on my own observation and that of people who have been in positions similar to mine—that, generally speaking, Presidents have most of the facts.

"It is all strangely reminiscent of the old days in Russia when the Russian peasants were saying: 'If the Czar only knew how we were living, the Holy Father would do something about it.' But the Czar did know; he just didn't give a damn because he had his own political program. And the same is true of Presidents."

The question of advisers was then discussed by Mr. Reedy: "The point has been raised of what happens when the President has Nobel prize winners advising him on an issue. The answer, of course, is that he will fire the two whose advice is contrary to his, and sustain the one whose advice goes along with his political predilections. This involves a somewhat broader political theory which applies not alone to a President but to politics generally.

"A President must be a supreme politician, and, like all politicians, must have an extraordinary capacity for adapting himself to factual situations.

"In the political arena facts, to a great extent, are not determining, but reinforcing. This can give rise to some melancholy thoughts, not quite so much about the nature of politicians, but about the metaphysical nature of reality."

Mr. Reedy was asked whether President Johnson had sufficient information on which to base sound judgment and specifically what information, if any, he needed and was not available to him.

Contrast in Meetings

"I think Mr. Johnson had all the information he needed," Mr. Reedy replied. "What he did not have—and it would have been invaluable—was the type of adversary debate that he might have had in the Senate. In '54 when Eisenhower asked Johnson, then majority leader, to check out what the reaction among the Senate Democrats would be if he went to the aid of the French at Dien Bien Phu, Johnson called a meeting of the Senate Democratic Policy Committee.

"In that meeting, everyone stood on a level. I was the only staff member there. And that is one debate I shall never forget. They pounded the table; they screamed at one another; they used short Anglo-Saxon words. That is the way men should act when they are talking about life and death.

"After all, this decision was to determine whether a lot of men were going to go out and wade around in the rice paddies. At the end of that session, Johnson went back and told Eisenhower he had better not try it because the roof would blow right off the Capitol dome.

"Years later, I found myself in the National Security Council. It was a calm, orderly debate; each man was sitting there, holding the cards close, watching the man next to him. All of the facts were there. What was missing was the fury that should go into political debate. It is not basically a question of information, but a question of contact and debate with fellow human beings."

Mr. Hyman recalled a similar case in the Senate, "the first hearings on outer space, when the learned Senators, all patriots, were sitting with Johnson. A succession of scientists came before them and the Senators were all nodding their heads sagely; they obviously didn't understand a word of what was being said, even though they were faced with a critical decision."

Mr. Reedy commented: "What happens over a period of time is that Presidential commitments become more irreversible. No man, once he has committed forces to battle, can ever say to himself—I made a mistake. I am not now talking about questions of egotism. Imagine waking up in the morning and trying to live with yourself if you had to say '15,000 men are dead, 20,000 men are dead, because I made a mistake.' I doubt whether any living being could do it."

And Now the "Ideal"

At one of the political panels these questions were put: What is the "ideal President" and have we had him and what would his qualifications be? Mr. Hyman responded first: "In considering the question—a most difficult question —of the 'ideal President' both old and new aspects need to be surveyed. In the past there have been quite a number of grounds for—I won't say cynicism—but unease about the Presidential office and the act of choice. In the first place, it is part of the glory and the terror of the Presidency that you never really know what you are going to get from a man who is a candidate until the materials of the office are turned over to him. Some men are equipped for every high office except the Presidency, while others are equipped for no office except the Presidency.

"There is a second ground for unease—and some cynicism I suppose—when you consider the choices we have made in the past. Sometimes it seems to me that, if you ever really want to get anything done or to achieve anything important in the Presidency, you ought to find a wrong man to stand for the right things for the wrong reasons.

"Because of the way we look at things these days, a man of that kind is safe. If he had the right reasons we would be very uneasy because the expectations would be high; whereas if he had the wrong reasons, if he was the wrong man but did the right thing, we would say, well, he really didn't mean what he said; all he wanted to do was get elected. If you had a right man standing for the right things for the right reasons, I feel reasonably sure that he would be crucified in short order as a subversive.

"Another cause for unease arises out of a study of Presidential histories. There seems to be a kind of a politics of reverse images in the performance of Presidents. It is as though a man we elect makes an appraisal of himself, worries that people might think there is something odd about him, and then proceeds to perform in a way precisely the opposite of the manner which his previous conduct might suggest.

"Thus, an aristocrat like Franklin Roosevelt becomes the voice of the dispossessed; a General-President like Eisenhower, instead of becoming a Caesar, becomes a pacifist; a Catholic like John F. Kennedy becomes more Protestant than Martin Luther; and an old vendettist like Richard Nixon for a while gives an impression of loving-kindness in such towering heights that one fears for the soles on the sandals of the Heavenly choir."

But Is There an "Ideal"?

Mr. Reedy questioned whether there is such a thing as an "ideal President." "I suppose somewhere along the line some genetic genius will be able to come up with a combination of St. Francis of Assisi, Aristotle, and Jim Farley. But pending that, I am very skeptical that there is such a person or that the ideal President can be even defined. Gary Wills, in his impressive book, said that the American people operate under the myth that their system produces the best man for the job. This, he said, is not true; what it does produce is a man appropriate for the job.

"I don't think we can employ the kind of job description used by industry or in the academic world and say: here are the qualities; now let's find the man to fit them. Because we do not have an infinity of choices, all political systems are complex and, somewhere along the line, choices have to be narrowed. Therefore, I'm afraid about the best we can do is to go ahead and vote and hope for the best."

Mr. Hyman then described the conundrum of the voter and offered some criteria he might find useful: "How do you judge a man? An election is an act of prophecy that the voter makes about the character of a President. Common instinct should tell you that what you are deciding today may not be valid tomorrow or the day after tomorrow or four years hence. A whole mass of problems and controversies, unforeseeable now, will surely arise.

"Is it possible, one asks, to misjudge a man's character, even if, in the campaign, he presents himself in his natural state without a theatrical mask? I answer yes, because the judgment is based on his appearance as a candidate and not on how he would act in the pressure chamber of the Presidency.

"Is it possible to misjudge a man's character, even if he has served in the Presidency for a term of years? Again I answer yes, because the stresses on him change from one term to another.

"Is it possible we may deceive ourselves in judging the

character of a President? I answer yes, because what we praise or censure in another man may not apply to the President. And is it possible for a President of sterling character, properly judged by a wise and virtuous electorate, to use his discretionary power unwisely? And I answer yes, because even a President who is morally fit for the company of saints is not immune from the danger of taking actions based on false facts which he has valid reason for believing to be true.

"Shouldn't there be pauses when we consider, for example, the discretionary power of the President in the use of nuclear weapons, or the power to make war without a declaration of war by the Congress? And I answer yes. All this adds up to a tremendous reason for concern.

Weighing the Alternatives

"Then you ask: What is the alternative? Somebody must be trusted or there will be no civil government, no society. Someone must be vested with discretionary powers in great matters of state. Who outside the Presidency can be trusted with these discretionary powers? A man superior to the President? In that case you put to that man the same questions you raise about the President. A committee above the President? If so, which committee, with what members elected by whom and responsible to whom?

"And so, after you examine all the alternatives, you come back to the President himself. Where discretionary power in the highest matters of state must be vested in somebody, it is best vested in one man, decidedly not a committee. The one man will remain, in Hamilton's language, the object of the jealousy and the watchfulness of the people, whereas in the case of a committee responsibility cannot be fixed."

Mr. Hyman set out a number of criteria that he said might reduce the chances of error in the selection of a President. "I would ask first whether the man communicates to you the conviction that his first duty is to explain himself and, in so doing, to respect the integrity of words. It is not accidental that the Bible says rather explicitly that in the beginning was the Word. Because if you corrupt the integrity of the word, you corrupt your vision of reality; and once you corrupt the vision of reality, you corrupt the modes of action which flow from that vision. Furthermore, if you corrupt the integrity of the word, you corrupt something fundamental in our whole democratic order, which is a government by speaking. And if you corrupt the means by which we communicate, you corrupt the whole process.

"A second criterion to be applied to a candidate is whether he recognizes that power and responsibility go hand in hand. To divorce the two, to act as if they belonged to separate worlds, is not constitutional government, but a system for administrative nihilism.

"A third criterion: Has the candidate any kind of historic sense? No man can attend to everything that happens in the office of the Presidency; he must discriminate between transient things which he should delegate to subordinates and deep-running things. If he has the historic sense, he will concentrate on the organic movements and not be concerned with a mass of trivia. A President should understand that he does not live only in one moment but that what he does today is not only a consequence of the past, but will have an impact extending into the farthest future."

The Presidents Ranked

Apologetically, the moderator asked the panelists to rank

the Presidents first, second, and third. Mr. Hyman spoke first: "I would select George Washington first, but on a plane of his own, quite separate from the rest. He deserves a high rank even if he did nothing more than establish the principle of civilian supremacy. Moreover he was without doubt an institution builder.

"As you move beyond the founding fathers, I would definitely put Lincoln first. He expanded the power of the Presidency and brought into it a highly important moral ingredient which will never be forgotten: that the President is not only the ultimate source of discipline, but also the ultimate source of clemency. I would place second Harry Truman from the standpoint of magnitude of achievement, and Franklin Roosevelt third.

Mr. Reedy offered a slightly different list:

"There is this problem: when you say the greatest, the greatest what? I am quite willing to put George Washington at the head, on the basis that Sydney Hyman did—the establishment of the precedence of civilian authority, plus the heavy need for a symbol to hold us together at that particular moment in our history.

"On the other hand, if we were in a different period, I would find other qualities I would rank above that. If I were to ask which President faced up to a fundamental crisis that threatened to destroy the nation, I would place Lincoln first and Washington second. I would rate Andrew Jackson pretty high. And I quite agree about Truman; I think his Presidency has more long-range implications for the country than Roosevelt's. On the other hand, Roosevelt mastered a crisis and Truman did not.

"It really is an impossible question to answer. I would say that we have had about ten Presidents, roughly, who should be ranked, as men, above the other 25. In terms of greatness, you should take those ten and decide in what slots they should be placed."

And so the discussion ended with this rebuke aimed at the moderator by Mr. Hyman: "In answer to the question, I find refuge in St. Augustine who was asked what God was doing before he created the heaven and the earth and the answer was, he was creating a hell for people who ask such questions."

* * * *

We are deeply concerned, in connection with the global crisis, about the President's role in fashioning foreign policy. That has become an issue of increasing controversy between the White House and Capitol Hill. It is the theme of the next chapter.

Chapter 6
WHITE HOUSE VS. HILL

The contest between President and Congress over the formulation of foreign policy is likely to have a profound effect on how that policy is made. In any case, the duel is on and the result uncertain.

The Constitution clearly makes foreign policy the responsibility of both the President and the Congress. The Executive is given the tasks of negotiating agreements with foreign nations, of appointing representatives abroad, and of commanding the armed forces of the nation in times both of war and of peace. The Congress is just as explicitly assigned a role in foreign policy; the Senate approves or rejects treaties that the Executive has negotiated and appointments that the President has made; the House of Representatives initiates legislation for funds for the armed forces, for military operations, for foreign aid, for Ameri-

82

can consulates and embassies abroad, and for intelligence-gathering assignments in other countries.

The Congress also has the power to regulate trade with other nations, to raise and support the army, to maintain naval forces, to make rules for the regulation of the armed forces, and to declare war.

Although the Congress has continued to exercise its constitutional powers, during the past two decades it has done so mainly in the form of drafting legislation that the Executive has requested, in approving and implementing agreements that the Executive has made with other nations, in granting military appropriations which the White House and Department of Defense have requested, and in backing military intervention initiated by the Executive.

Since 1951 the United States has been involved in two major wars and has sent troops to Lebanon, to the Dominican Republic, to Laos and Cambodia, and not once during this period has Congress declared war or even been consulted until after the disposition of troops. (The passage of the War Powers Bill now limits the President's power to commit troops abroad for extended periods—legislation that resulted from the failure of five succeeding Presidents to consult with Congress before sending armed forces abroad.)

During the past decade there has been a breakdown in communication between the Executive and the Congress in the area of foreign affairs. The classification of information by the Executive and the withholding of information on grounds of "executive privilege" (specific grants of silence) by the administrations have made it difficult for the Congress to exercise its prerogative of legislative oversight or to advise or consent to policies with any degree of knowledge.

Over the years the Congress has gradually yielded its power in foreign affairs to the President, for a number of reasons: first, because it is not greatly interested; second, because the problems are too complicated; third, because it does not have the information, and fourth and most important, if something goes wrong—for example, if war results—then the blame is on the Executive and not on the Congress. As a result, even though he is the leader of a democracy, the President has been acting more or less like a monarch in the area of foreign policy.

Does "Papa Know Best"?

Mr. Salisbury deplores the consequences: "There is a tendency which has become more and more apparent and which has been encouraged by a number of Presidents and Secretaries of State—a tendency best summed up as a 'Papa knows best' formula. The argument goes that if we only knew what the President knows with his access to all the secrets of the world, we wouldn't question his decisions—'Don't question what's going on in Washington because they [the government experts] know better.' Well, I am cynical enough to believe that anyone in this country who really wants to learn about 99.44% of the factors that go into any Presidential decision has them available through the *New York Times* and other newspapers, through *Time* Magazine and the broadcasting companies. The information is there; probably there is a small amount that nobody knows about except the President and perhaps Kissinger, but I don't believe much of this is vital.

"I'm afraid that the public, generally speaking, takes the view that, after all, foreign affairs are complex. We don't know the names of all the countries; we don't know the players. It isn't like turning on the tube and watching basketball or football or baseball.

"It bothers me enormously that people seem to feel paralyzed when it comes to understanding foreign policy; that they think there is some huge and wonderfully competent foreign-policy apparatus in Washington, but that they themselves are little people, unable to understand the intricacies of foreign affairs or to question the experts. It reminds me too much of the attitude of the Russians in those long years when I was in Russia—the Czars were far and distant but very wise men who knew all.

"The Czar never was a very wise man, and he didn't know all, and our Presidents, although certainly rather wise, have not had a monopoly on wisdom. I think it's about time, considering the fact that occasionally they have made mistakes in foreign policy, that we show our interest. If it happens that our ideas follow along the same lines as those of the President and the Secretaries of State, then we can strongly reinforce their policies because, as citizens, we are able to exert our influence through our representatives and senators."

Mr. Lewis agreed: "I'm glad that Harrison mentioned the tendency to look to Washington and the tendency for people in Washington to think they know best. I think it's important to emphasize that what has happened in recent years is not something new under the sun. Nicholas Katzenbach has made a point of showing that the same kind of policy-making in secret resulted in disaster in the Kennedy administration. He uses the example of the Bay of Pigs to show how an attempt to carry off a tremendously important foreign-policy maneuver without any open discussion was disastrous."

Congress Is Speaking Up

The situation is now changing. There is developing a determination in Congress to reassert its constitutional prerogative, a feeling that certain policies were wrong or at least should have been subject to close examination. For, fundamentally, foreign policy has been made by a two-man team—a procedure that has brought the charges of "dictatorship."

Mr. Semple sees it this way: "We need leadership, not arrogance. The President should be willing to reach out and consult. Presidents have been conceded too much, and they have developed contempt for the rest of the system. The real issue before us is: Can we get a President who will level with the people? We have been going through a period in which our Presidents have done all sorts of insane things—subverting governments under the guise of keeping us safe, Vietnam, Watergate. These all indicate that we have to demand access. The Congress and the people have allowed the President to operate in this way."

Professor Strum agreed with Mr. Semple. The President, she said, is the leader of a democracy. "He is not a king, and he should remember that the President is only one institution among many." Professor Padover warned that "the President has become an institution dangerous to American liberties. The basic question is how do we maintain strong leadership without letting the President become a dictator in the role of foreign affairs. Congress has abdicated its powers. The President has moved into the vacuum." Whether Mr. Ford will modify the Nixon-Kissinger method will soon be answered.

The Executive has been reacting sharply to these moves in the Congress. Secretary Kissinger warned in a recent speech against the "grave issues" raised by the growing tendency of Congress to legislate in detail the day-to-day or week-to-week conduct of our foreign affairs: "American policy must be a coherent and purposeful whole. The way we act in our relations with one country almost inevitably affects our relationship with others. To single out individual countries for special legislative attention has unintended but inevitable consequences and risks unraveling the entire fabric of our foreign policy. . . . Paradoxically, the President and the Congress share the same immediate objectives on most of the issues that have recently become sources of dispute. Too often differences as to tactics have defeated the very purposes that both branches meant to serve, because the legislative sanctions were too public or too drastic or too undiscriminating."

Nevertheless, the recent actions of Congress to which Mr. Kissinger alludes resulted from a sense among Congressmen and Senators that the policies being pursued by the Administration were wrong. More than that, these actions reflect a growing impatience with Mr. Kissinger's tendency to conduct much of the nation's foreign policy in secret.

How Congress Could Help

Assuming that the Congress reasserted its authority in foreign affairs, what function could it perform? Mr. Pool observed that Congress is very important as a check upon the Presidency "because it is one place where public opinion registers. . . . We need a loud, vociferous Congress to control the purse strings, even though it can't administer policy." He stressed, however, that Congress is not necessarily the antidote. "Four-hundred-and-fifty members cannot act as a decision-making body, although they are good at recognizing mistakes, and Congressmen don't want to make decisive decisions—only to follow the usual process of legislation."

Professor Hyman also considers the Congress a check against the absolute power of the President: "One of the ways of controlling the Presidency is to see to it that the Congress performs its proper functions as a legislature—which means the functions of supervision of the acts of the Executive. This means that what we call the function of oversight has to be upgraded, and the function, the simple function of drafting legislation, has to be examined. And I would attack the problem by sloughing away from the Congress so many of the day-to-day activities, which simply keep an average member from thinking about his job as a legislator; he becomes everything except that; he is an errand boy. [No] matter how serious he is, he does not have time to think about the problems of government."

Mr. Reedy said that the Congress could do a great deal to help the public gain some understanding of the facts of foreign policy. "The editor, from a Constitutional standpoint, should be the Congress, so the question becomes: How can you make Congress assume the job of supplementing the information given out by the President, challenging that information, even challenging the authority of the President, because he is the one who commands the attention? Then you have to do something about the Congress as well as the Presidency."

Dr. Fatemi felt that under the present system Congress is not mobilized or equipped to act as a check upon the President "because it does not have enough information in the area of foreign relations. The Congress must set up a body of expert advisers from outside to advise it the same way that the President has his own advisers. I think both the Foreign Relations Committee of the Senate and the Foreign Affairs Committee of the House are especially in need of such expert help. The Congressman has too much work to do, and his assistants are, for the most part, political appointees who are not expert in these fields."

Mr. Holt felt that the Senate should act as a forum for the debate of foreign-policy issues. However, in many cases when it has performed this function, it has attracted little attention. "Committee hearings should be more frequently televised," he says. But, he cautions, "You can have 'equal time' until it's coming out of your ears, and it doesn't do any good if people don't tune in."

In such a debate, the President has all the advantages. He can appeal to the public in two important ways: through television addresses and through press conferences. As for the first, the President has the right of unlimited access to prime time. That makes opposition difficult, because the opponents do not get equal prominence, or equal time in rejoinder.

Nor does the press conference prove satisfactory. It is, of course, a unique American institution, a sort of symbol— even though kind of meretricious—of democracy; here is the head of a great state permitting himself to be subjected to questioning by reporters. But it is a kind of catch-as-catch-can performance and could be much more illuminating if the correspondents didn't treat it like a bull-ring performance. Television is the big act—either in "fireside chats" or press conferences. The electronic age has transformed these performances, putting charm ahead of substance.

Presidents as TV Stars

The history of Presidential appeals to the public provides fascinating insights into character. Franklin Roosevelt's predecessors had used the radio sparingly. He developed it into a genuine instrument of propaganda and persuasion. But, like Kennedy, he had a fear of overexposure.

Incidentally, Lyndon Johnson had no such fear, so confident was he of what he considered his particular brand of homespun charisma.

Truman was the first President to use television to any degree, both for direct talks with the nation and for his press conferences. But he did not exploit the medium to the full. It was left to Eisenhower to do so and he mustered all the advertising agency tricks and all the technical stunts to make it effective. (He called Robert Montgomery as his adviser and he carefully prepared his TV addresses. He used to say he tried to look sincere on television; he had a monitor close at hand and when he felt he might seem insincere, he changed his expression.) All the technical details were taken care of; for example, his speeches were written out in large type so that he did not have to use glasses to read them.

The real performer, however, was Kennedy. His words were carefully selected and dramatically delivered. There is a story about the famous inaugural address. Somehow it had sounded like the Gettysburg Address. We checked with his secretary, Ted Sorensen, who reported that yes, they had analyzed the Gettysburg Address and consciously attempted to make the Kennedy address both sparse and effective. For example, they discovered that out of 336 words in the Lincoln inaugural, some 300 were single-syllable words and they tried to use that mathematical formula.

Johnson used TV frequently but he was not too persuasive a performer; Nixon was artificial and unconvincing; Ford has a year to polish his TV skills. The opposition has had no such facilities or opportunities. They may get equal time—at an off-hour and with full competition from other programs.

Most of the analysts felt that Presidential power had to be checked by both the Congress and public opinion, that it should not be absolute. "A more democratic foreign policy" —that is the basic aim. Which means that the people, voting through the Congress, shall make their voices heard. But they must express informed opinion—or there is the danger that we will succumb to propaganda or demagogy.

PART III:
OPINION OR EMOTION?

Of the two essential elements needed to produce a sound foreign policy, the first—leadership—has been dissected in Part II. In these chapters the second ingredient—public opinion—is surveyed. It is a subject deep in linguistic mists; almost everybody talks about it, but no one is sure what it is. As part of the discussion, the attitudes and the knowledge of the public are explored and the performance of the media is appraised.

Chapter 7
WHAT IS IT?

What then does the phrase *public opinion* connote? Even though the phrase defies definition, it is constantly used by the politicians, the pollsters and the prognosticators in general. It is, moreover, the acid test of genuine democracy.

In an effort to arrive at fundamentals, questionnaires were sent to a group of well-known public figures. They were asked how they would define public opinion. Most of them ducked definite answers. Among the responses were these:

Reedy: "Public opinion is a consensus of individual attitudes of sufficient size to initiate, influence, sustain, diminish, or block social action. It is never monolithic, but is best considered in terms of vectoring as practiced by physicists, a collection of forces veering in the same direction and mutually influencing each other."

Graff: "Public opinion is the least common denominator of the people's attitude on this or that."

Graber: "I like to define public opinion as publicly expressed views about current issues of wide public concern held by representative groups of people and presumably derived from public discussion of these issues."

Bradlee: "I would define public opinion as what a definable segment of the American people thinks it knows at any given time. Public opinion should be mistrusted since there are so many publics and they have such ill-defined opinions."

Lewis: "Public opinion is the body of belief in the community on any issue. In foreign affairs it may often be only informed opinion that one considers, since many are neither informed nor interested."

Crotty: "I think of public opinion in empirical terms — who holds what views on what issues with what degree of intensity. I think it is a subtle, fractionated distribution of impulses."

Gallagher: "I would define public opinion as that point at which the majority of the public agree on a single point of view on any given subject."

Davison: "Public opinion is a consensus involving substantial numbers of individual opinions on a public issue."

Gallup: "Many persons have tried to define public opinion. The simplest definition is 'the sum total of individual views' or, as James Bryce said, 'the aggregate of views men hold regarding matters that affect or interest the community.' "

Bailey: "Public opinion is the opinion at a given time of the public at large, excluding those who have no opinion on a given subject and including press opinion, pressure group opinion, and so forth. Press opinion must not be confused with public opinion. Public opinion is often held privately and frequently not voiced."

Mannes: "Public opinion is a doubtful consensus of a splintered plurality as derived by polls of 'average' Americans in all walks of life. Actually, the expression of a syncopated chorus who think that they know what they think."

Bagdikian: "That collection of attitudes and beliefs held by members of the public in various degrees of intensity at different times and with variant configurations at different times and issues which at any point of decision may crystallize to the point where it can be tested or express itself in some outward behavior."

Burns: "Clusters of attitudes on the part of the mass public, as mobilized by leaders and structured by political, economic, and social institutions."

Frankel offers an interesting division: "There is an 'inner harbor' of public opinion—knowledgeable and influential people who are not directly involved in making the decisions; an 'outer harbor'—influential people who have 'clout' over a wide range of issues; and finally more general opinion, which shows up in votes, polls, collective moods, etcetera."

Brzezinski: "Broadly shared or highly generalized views on issues of common concern, usually without too much expert knowledge."

Public opinion, one concludes, can be a real force even though it is indefinable, because it represents the consensus of disparate groups. Note the "can be," because it often fails to take form.

The Opinion Process

The forces that contribute (or could contribute) to the formation of public opinion are of two kinds; one might well be called the exterior forces, which are outside influences; the others are the interior forces, which operate for the most part subconsciously.

The outside influences are easily identified: the Presidency, the Congress, the media, the public groups, the educational institutions. The inside—almost subliminal—forces have much more impact than they are usually given credit for—the habits of thought and the standards of conduct that result from the kind of life a person leads, the neighbors with whom he chats, the gabble he hears, the sort of movies he sees—in general what one might call the social milieu.

Mr. Webster remarked that television programs and motion pictures have more impact than the news media in forming emotional rather than logical images. "Television and films are media of experience, not of explanation. I have a sneaking suspicion that the attitudes in this country toward Britain are affected as much by British serials as they are by the reports which appear in the news columns. This is very worrisome, for it works both ways; our attitudes toward America can be conditioned from watching hours of 'Cannon,' 'Mannix,' and 'The Waltons.' "

The outer influences are those designed to influence intelligence or to rouse enthusiasm or indignation, but the inner forces are often the determining factor; one wonders whether the politicians take enough account of these.

There is rarely such a thing as a majority public opinion—which implies that there is a majority of the country in favor of a particular course. Such examples of consensus were seen in the ultimate judgments about Vietnam and Watergate, but they are infrequent. One might have expected Vietnam to lead to a strong isolationist sentiment, a determination not to take part in adventures abroad. That

was true for a while but then came international compli-
cations, notably the oil crisis and with it the realization
that we were part of the world. As for Watergate, other
matters have overshadowed it.

Basic Fact: Ignorance

There is this all-important fact about public opinion in
the area of foreign affairs: Despite its fundamental character, despite the debates that whirl around it, opinion is
generally uninformed and volatile.

The evidence of this ignorance is abundant. The pollsters
estimate that less than 2% of the population is fully knowledgeable about foreign affairs, and that only 15% show any
interest in international news. Moreover, the views expressed are often contradictory. For example, on the one
hand the country on the whole has accepted détente; on
the other hand, one out of two Americans thinks that
American communism is an immediate and present danger.

We did a survey of members of Congress who had served
on the foreign relations committees of both houses. Of the
16 who responded, there was not one who felt that the
public was "well informed" about foreign affairs without
qualification. Five reported that they considered it "poorly"
or "not too well informed." Ten felt that their constituents were "relatively well informed." Congressman Burke
said, "they are informed as well as the media cover news
events," which, according to the media experts, is a dubious compliment.

Another example of ignorance: pollees were asked, "Can
you recall offhand where the right of the free press in this
country comes from; that is, on what is it based?" Forty-
five percent said the Constitution; 3% the Declaration of
Independence; 52% gave other sources or had no opin-

ion. If the Constitution was mentioned, they were asked in what part; only 12% said the Bill of Rights; 7% said the First Amendment; the rest said they didn't know.

This is how Secretary Kissinger summed up the situation: "I do not think the country—if one may presume to think about what the country thinks—has the vaguest idea of what it is being called upon to do in foreign affairs. We have to tell the American people what they are called upon to do. That is our biggest problem; it is our biggest challenge right now.

"I think in foreign policy we need a national understanding of what is needed, what is meant by peace, and an understanding that we are living in a world in which peace cannot be imposed on others, which means that sometimes the outcomes must be less than perfect. So we have to know what we mean by peace; we have to know what we mean by cooperation; we have, above all, to understand these big issues which we have been discussing, like energy and food, in which our actions will crucially determine what happens in the rest of the world."

Profile of the Voter

Further light on the voter was provided by Mr. Yankelovich, who reported: "There are three prime facts to keep in mind in considering the electorate. In 1968, about 71% of the eligible public registered and 61% of the eligible public—at that time some 120 million—turned out to vote.

"This was a continuation of a long-term trend—a slow but steady decline in turnout. Four years before, the turnout rate was 63%; four years before that, 64%; at the turn of the century it was 80%. Many a textbook has been written in political science on the meaning of that slow erosion. It is certainly shrouded in mystery as far as the past is concerned, but it is an important point at the present time. [The figure for the '72 election turnout is 55%.]

"The second fact is that those who participate in voting to the greatest degree are influenced by age and education. The highest voting participation is found among men, among people between the ages of 45 and 64, white, of higher education and income, white collar and professional and managerial. The lowest has been among women, among young people to a lesser extent, among old people, blacks, Southerners, people of low income and low education.

"As for age, keeping in mind that the turnout average is 61%, the 21-to-24-year-old group is at about a 51% level, whereas in the 35-to-75 group, it is at about a 75% level. The youth vote deserves particular scrutiny. There are 25 million potentially new voters this year, the 18-to-24-year-old group. Seven out of ten are not in school. The 30% in-school group turn out at a very high 66–67% rate; they have, therefore, a disproportionate voting influence. The lowest of all turnouts is among young people not in school —about 40%.

"Now, very quickly, a third well-known fact: There are more Democrats than Republicans. Our latest survey, and this varies a great deal, indicates that 45% of the electorate is Democratic, 29% Republican, and 26% independent."

The next step in arriving at a profile of the voter was to examine him according to political orientation. Mr. Yankelovich continued: "In one area of our polling we asked people to characterize themselves as conservatives, moderates, or liberals in their viewpoint.

"About one year ago, 20% of the voters said that they thought of themselves as liberals, 51%, moderate or middle-of-the-road, and 26%, conservative. Today this is the picture: There is no real change in the number of liberals, but the moderate, middle-of-the-road group is down to 34% and the conservative up to 41%. (The total is not 100 because some people would not characterize themselves.)

"This is really a very great change. Whereas a year ago liberals and conservatives balanced each other out, now the liberals are outnumbered two to one, and the conservatives now constitute the single largest group.

"When in 1972 you asked people the important question of how they see the candidates, about 61% of the voting public saw McGovern as either liberal or radical and only about 19% saw him as moderate or conservative."

Efforts to Define

Mr. Yankelovich's designations were sharply questioned. He was asked whether any attempt had been made to discover from the people who were polled how they defined the words *conservative* and *liberal*. He replied:

"We did not attempt to get any semantic definition of the words, but we did try to check these self-descriptions with questions designed to establish the real beliefs. It is as though, when you are questioning someone who says he is a police officer, you ask him to show you his badge. You say: "Let's see what your views are." Those who say they are conservative hold a whole set of views ranging from busing and pornography to the candidate himself; it's a very familiar set of viewpoints.

"I'll give you one example. Certainly one of the elements in the conservative viewpoint is an anti-social-welfare attitude. Many of these people are strapped for money; they feel the pinch on their pocketbooks very tightly; and they go from that feeling to the conclusion that the reason for their trouble is not defense or other expenditures, but the cost of welfare. They ask: 'Why should I knock myself out and work hard for some bum who isn't willing to work for himself?' This is a growing feeling and it is also a reaction against 'liberal' criticisms of traditional values."

Mr. Reedy offered a footnote: "If you ever made a survey of the United States to look into the many different versions of *liberal* and *conservative,* I think you might be very surprised. There are places in the United States where the word *liberal* means that a greater amount of oil is allowed to be taken out of the ground and the word *conservative* means greater spacing of oil wells so not quite so much oil can be pumped out.

"I have had quite a bit of experience in politics around the country and I have very, very grave doubts about any question that merely asks: Are you 'conservative' or 'liberal?' "

Miss Friedan added: "The words *liberal, radical,* and *conservative* do not mean very much any more because, as events change, so do people's thoughts and feelings."

Mr. Yankelovich again defined the terms. "At best, the words are awkward shorthand. They mean a lot of things. There are places where the word *liberal* means being practical in the spending of money. The semantics are what are at issue. I could use other words, but these are meaningful in the sense that they represent a measurable change.

"When you look at the beliefs of people who call themselves 'conservative' or 'liberal,' very different patterns emerge. Those who consider themselves 'liberal' feel that we have not had enough change and that change should be more rapid; the people who consider themselves 'conservative' feel that things have changed too much. The 'conservatives' think we are doing too much for the minorities; the 'liberals' say that we are doing too little for the minorities. You can go down a list of 20 or 30 or 40 beliefs and you discover that they have some kind of common denominator, some kind of definition—in that sense, they are meaningful.

"One has to distinguish very sharply between members of the Conservative Party and people who call themselves conservatives. The 41% who call themselves conservatives are actually split half and half between Republicans and Democrats. For the mass of people who now think of their attitudes as being a little more conservative than they were a year ago, the tradition of anti-communism persists in the country.

"I was rather surprised to find the extent to which the Vietnam War is interpreted by the mass of people as part of the chess game, part of the cold war. The cold war may have diminished in Washington, but you can't turn the country around like a kiddie car, and the country still persists in its anti-communist attitude. And they think Mr. Nixon was being very clever in that he recognized the opportunity to play China against Russia, and Russia against China, and the like.

"The fact remains that whatever people may mean by these words, there has been a huge change in a year's time, due either to changes of definition or changes of attitude on the part of the people. One or the other has to be the case."

A Dissenting View

Mr. Reedy disagreed: "No, not at all. I think it's rather that Mr. Nixon had been catching up; his political positions changed significantly in the last couple of years because he sensed a growing conservative mood. As a result, he modified the programs he sent to Congress, the character of his vetoes, and all the rest. He conformed to a changing mood in the country, not vice-versa.

"It is not a one-way street. Leadership has an effect; it reinforces certain points of view people hold. There is undoubtedly a relationship between leadership and people, but this does not mean that the people have changed. I contend that the Nixon view changed. In order to be convinced of it you have only to look at the masses of data that show that when you go below the surface you discover what people believe.

"It doesn't make any sense to ask people to give you a semantic definition of the term. Most people aren't too careful about their use of words or too clear about their concepts. But if you determine what they really believe, you can arrive at a very good operational definition of the terms."

The composition of the two parties was discussed by a number of the speakers. There seemed to be general agreement that while they were different in objective and constituency, nevertheless neither was really representative of the composition of the public.

The differences were emphasized by Mr. Yankelovich: "Neither the Republican nor the Democratic party provides a cross section of the public. From a demographic point of view, they are very different, not only in their ideology and political beliefs, but also in the basic demographic facts. The Democrats are heavily weighted in the direction of Catholics, Jews, and young people, and the Republicans are very heavily Protestant, upper-income, better educated, older. The independents appeal to a very high proportion of young people who renounce the idea of party loyalty.

"An interesting sidelight is that from 1952 until the 1972 election there has not been a presidential election in which there has not been a Catholic majority for the Democrats. A majority of Catholics voted for Adlai Stevenson, for Humphrey, for Johnson, for whoever the candidate was. Nixon made large inroads into the usual Democratic vote among the Catholics, the low-income people, and young people with low levels of education. On the whole it has been a dramatic reversal of the historical pattern."

Mr. Hyman ended the discussion with these devastating bons mots: "These politics of reverse images in a way obscure, if you want to be cynical about it, one of the fundamental differences between the Republican and the Democratic parties. If I never write another line in my life, never have another thought in my life, I shall be content on my deathbed to say that I finally did discover the basic distinction between the two parties, which is this: The Democrats are a large group of second-class roughnecks led by a small group of first-class aristocrats; whereas the Republicans are a small group of second-class aristocrats, led by a rather large group of first-class roughnecks."

*   *   *   *

If democracy depends on public opinion and public opinion rarely registers its views (if it has views) in foreign policy, what measure have we of sentiment? The polls, say the pollsters. They are examined in the next chapter.

Chapter 8
SAMPLING THE POLLS

The polls, which have assumed a large role in the political process, were debated and analyzed, defended and attacked at several of the sessions.

Dr. Gallup offered the primary interpretation of—and justification for—the surveys: "In setting forth the rationale of polls I would like first of all to make this distinction. There are two kinds of polls: election polls and polls on issues of the day. I believe that issue polls are far more important than election polls. However, for the media and those in political life, polls on candidates' standing hold far more interest than issue polls and receive much more attention; in fact, many persons think of polls only in relation to elections.

"Now what are some of the uses of polls? First of all, polls make it possible for the people to communicate with their representatives. No matter how much the urging, only a tiny fraction of the public bothers to keep in contact with their representatives in the Congress or in the state legislatures; and the ones who do invariably represent the articulate minority. In fact, in the absence of polls, pressure groups can and do make all kinds of wild claims. The National Rifle Association can still keep gun legislation off the books, but at least legislators know how their constituents feel on the issue.

"Polling is merely an instrument for gauging public opinion. When a President or any other leader pays attention to poll results, he is being alerted to the views of the people. Any other interpretation is nonsense. One might as well insist that a thermometer makes the weather, or that a microscope should be held accountable for the bacteria its lens reveals.

"Polls serve government in many ways—federal, state, and local government. All are making greater use of polls every year for both policy and administrative purposes, to make government more efficient and more responsive to the will of the people.

"Many critics overlook the simple truth that no better way has ever been found to discover the views of the public than the survey or polling method. Members of the Congress can read their mail from constituents, can follow the editorials in the newspapers and the views expressed by columnists and commentators on the air, can visit their home districts every weekend, but they can not know how their people feel without talking to a true cross section of their constituents; in short, by taking their own private polls.

"I remember a conversation I had with Mr. Truman. He said that he did not need a public-opinion poll to know how the people in the state of Missouri or any other place felt. So I said, 'Well, how do you do it then, Mr. President?' And he said, 'Well, what I do is to go out and talk to them, people in all walks of life.' And I said, 'Well, you were, in effect, taking a poll.' It had never really occurred to him that he was, in effect, doing what we all do, except that we do it more systematically than any one person could.

"Well, it can, of course, be argued that each member of the Congress should sit in his own little ivory tower and refuse to pay attention to the views of the electorate and be guided only by his conscience. This situation could hardly be described as democratic, and certainly it would not appeal to candidates who think constantly about getting reelected. The basic question, I repeat, is not whether the leader is paying too much attention to polls, but whether he is paying enough attention to the views of the people."

A member of the audience put this direct question to Mr. Yankelovich: "How accurate are the polls? Can we trust them?"

Elements of Doubt

Mr. Yankelovich replied: "I don't think you should trust the polls. This isn't a joke. Let me make myself very clear. The polls reflect what people say today but they say nothing about what people are going to do tomorrow. And very often people don't do tomorrow what they say they believe today.

"Where the polls have some degree of scientific status is in the sampling methods. That has reached a pretty high level, so that you can be reasonably sure that if you have the right kind of sample—1500 to 2000 people—it will represent the country as a whole. But then you can turn around and ask those same people a lot of stupid questions that are not at all scientific, and the result will be a lot of biased or misleading information.

"In ancient Rome they used to cut up sick chickens and look at their entrails. Well, at least the present method is cleaner, even if it may not be more accurate."

Some of the non-pollsters had reservations, Mr. Reedy for example: "Listening to Dr. Gallup, I suddenly realized that one of the main problems, when we discuss polls, is that there is a question here which goes beyond polls themselves. I find myself highly impressed with the way pollsters have developed their particular art. But when we apply it to the political world all of a sudden red flags start rising and bells start ringing and I have the feeling that the polls are being discussed as in a vacuum and the political process is not being analyzed in its true context.

"Take one specific example that has been cited—the activity of the National Rifle Association and the reasons congressmen go on voting against gun controls regardless of the polls. Dr. Gallup ascribes it to the political campaign contributions that come in from the National Rifle Association. I believe you could abolish those contributions and you could make the National Rifle Association utterly impotent, and those congressmen would not change their votes, because the political problem is more complex than finding out just how people feel about a specific issue.

"The congressman wants to know, first of all, how intense that feeling is. He knows that if he votes for gun controls, the people who are for gun controls will judge him on the basis of a range of issues. He also knows that the people who are against gun controls are going to vote against him if he votes for gun controls, no matter how well he satisfies them on other issues."

This question was put: If a poll only represents the point of view of today, then should not the media and the pollsters make it clear that something may happen; that some of these people who are Democrats may, at the last minute, balk at voting Republican? There are few such warnings in any of the stories written about the polls.

Mr. Yankelovich responded. "It isn't for lack of trying on the part of the polling people; they don't want to be caught in that kind of foolishness, because what they are doing is valuable and scientific in its own right. The press, however, looks upon the thing as a horseman's kind of sport. The predictions are of great interest to the media—and presumably to the public—but they jeopardize the scientific standing of the public opinion profession. So we make the qualifications; most of the time they do appear, but people don't seem to read them."

Impact of the Polls

The question of the influence of the polls—beneficent or evil—was fully explored.

Mr. Yankelovich said he would "inventory these kinds of influences that I have seen either at first or secondhand: first, an influence on campaign contributions, both in primaries and in national elections. Second, an influence on volunteers; if your man is way behind, it is awfully difficult to get up any kind of passion and commitment. Third, a probable influence on whether people do or do not vote—which works both ways; those who support the candidate who seems to be way ahead figure: 'Why should we bother? He doesn't need our vote,' while those who feel that they are with a loser may be demoralized.

"Dr. Gallup and many others have pointed out how, over the years, this so-called bandwagon effect has not worked, because the historical pattern is for a person who is behind to close the gap. If there were a bandwagon effect, it should be the very opposite. The gap would grow larger and larger. Now that implies that there may be a sympathy, underdog type of effect and there is some evidence of this."

The moderator pressed Mr. Yankelovich to answer the question: Is all this good or bad? This was Mr. Yankelovich's reply. "I have been waffling back and forth on that question for a long time. There is an assumption that the average voter, as soon as he sees that so-and-so is a winner, is going, like sheep, to vote for him. That's not the case; my experience has been that people take their vote for the President very, very seriously, and I would be willing to wager that there is virtually no one in this room whose decision to vote for one or the other candidate has been influenced by a bandwagon effect of the polls.

"In that sense the President is not a package of cigarettes or a can of beer. In our market-research work, we know that the bandwagon effect works, that if a product is popular its popularity is enhanced by having the look of a leader. Thank God, it doesn't carry over to political elections. People don't react that way. They make up their minds. I don't see why the average person should not have this input of information available to him, to use as he sees fit.

"From that point of view, I think it is perfectly consistent with the democratic posture to believe that this influence is, by and large, not a bad thing. Now at least, I have stated a position. I say that (a) the polls have an influence and (b) that it's not bad."

The "Me-Too" Vote

Dr. Gallup added then, "Well, let me say, first of all,

that I never in my polling career have seen any hard evidence to indicate that people are decisively influenced by polling results. I would agree that probably they do dry up some of the very sizable gifts made by a few individuals to a candidate for the purpose of buying or seeking favor. But that does not disturb me very much. People do take their votes very seriously; and if that were not the case, there would be no minority parties anywhere. In many countries there are as many as fifteen parties; if everyone wanted to be on the winning side, how could this happen?

"As to whether the polls are a good or bad influence, I cannot answer that, simply because I have yet to see an influence at work. Polling reports a substantial amount of legitimate news, just as does any other kind of political reporting."

Dr. Lazarsfeld said there were two effects of polls that counteract each other: "Some people, if they see that a candidate is ahead, decide to vote for him; other people who see the same polls decide to vote against the candidate; thus the net effect of the polls is a noneffect. I think the paradox is charming. The people do use information, but they use it differently.

"On the other hand, I have not the slightest doubt that campaign contributions are affected by polls. And it might well be that the activity of volunteers might be affected by them."

The discussion turned to the question of how much attention a President should pay to the polls.

This was Mr. Yankelovich's view: "Even though they provide useful pieces of information, I think that if polls govern the decision of the President, the man does not belong in that office. One of the reasons why a President is granted tenure for at least four years is to enable him to resist public opinion. It is spelled out in the Federalist Papers, in which Hamilton talks about the importance of having a man with the courage and the magnanimity to advance the highest interests of the nation even though the momentary displeasure of the people is incurred. Hamilton observes how often it happens that monuments of gratitude are raised in after years to men who display that courage and magnanimity.

"The question is: What constitutes Presidential courage in resisting public opinion, and what constitutes bullheadedness? It is a very narrow line. But if we understand our system, we realize that one of the reasons the President has the veto power is to resist public opinion and to resist the combined strength of two-thirds of the Congress.

"Now, these powers of resistance—tenure, a fixed term of office, and the rest of it—are almost like a knife; in the hands of a criminal it can take life; in the hands of a surgeon it can save life. We should be concerned with the abuse of these Presidential controls, rather than the abuse of Presidential power. I do not think we should take power away from the President."

Presidents and Polls

Mr. Reedy agreed that polls should be taken as indicators of public opinion at the moment. "And I go back to my basic thesis that information is used by a politician to reinforce rather than determine a position he takes.

"I can recall one period when one of the Presidents for whom I worked could not be approached for two minutes without his pulling ten polls out of his pocket. He even slipped one to me one time in church, when the Host was coming, and I felt a nudge and a poll was being shoved into my hand. Two years later the pollsters were all obviously idiots and didn't know what they were doing. You can't run government by polls. Anyway, I think that will always be the attitude.

"There is the question of what role public opinion should play in the President's decisions. I think that any President who looks at the polls and then runs like hell to get ahead of the masses would be the world's worst executive. On the other hand I think a President who is not aware of the inner psychological makeup of his constitutents is overlooking an important point. When a President is making policy of any kind, foreign or domestic, he must first survey the resources of the United States. And one of those resources consists of the attitude of the people toward a policy.

"I have the feeling that if Lincoln had taken a poll of the nation at a certain point in his Presidency and abided by its findings, he would have pulled out of the Civil War. But what Lincoln had was an inner knowledge of the resiliency of the American people and a realization of how far they were willing to go and how much they were willing to sacrifice.

"The President who ignores the real spiritual resources or the real makeup of the people, and considers only how they feel at the moment, if he ignores the fact that you can not make the people do certain things, that is as bad as swinging like a weathervane.

"The problem with the polls is that they do not reveal these spiritual values; they do not tell you how people will react when the ultimate choice is put to them. I say this even though I respect the polls."

Dr. Gallup commented, "I think polls provide legitimate

information for a President. What does he do with it? He should make up his mind independently of the polls, based on his own judgment. Now suppose he decides that busing is a good thing. But he has to understand why so many people are against it.

"Visualize a couple that moves out to the suburbs, having saved and scraped and sacrificed so that their kids would be able to go to a better school. Then comes a proposal that their kids be bused to some inferior school. This is seen by these people almost as an instrument of the devil. Unless you understand, therefore, how people feel and why they feel. you cannot devise sound programs for action.

"Nixon dealt with this very issue. 'The rights of each minority must be vigorously defended,' he said, 'and each minority must be protected in the opportunity to have its opinions become accepted as the majority view. But on these basic concerns the majority view must prevail, and leadership in the democracy is required to respond to that view.'

"Does this mean that a President should read all the public opinion polls before he acts, and then follow the opinion of the majority down the line? Of course not. A leader must be willing to take unpopular stands when they are necessary, but a leader who insists on imposing on the people his own idea of how they should live their lives, when those ideas go directly contrary to the values of the people themselves, does not understand the role of a leader in a democracy. And when he does find it necessary to take an unpopular stand, he has an obligation to explain it to the people. solicit their support, and win their approval."

The election poll stirs up large controversy. What social purpose, it was asked, does it serve?

The Election Polls

Dr. Gallup answered, "I can say with the deepest feeling that I wish we could give up election polling. It is costly, it serves no great social good, it brings criticism and, frankly, it's hard on our nerves. Now, we have not been able to give it up because the demand is there. We are not supported by the government or by a foundation but must get our support from the newspapers that report our findings—and they like election polls.

"Looking back over these nearly four decades of election polling, I conclude that this nerve-wracking operation has served one important purpose: It has made us examine carefully our research procedures and improve our methods every year. The pressure to be right is overwhelming. The researcher, the pollster, stands naked before the whole world the day after the election.

"Then there are the independent voters who constitute nearly a third of the electorate. They have no spokesman, no way to communicate with the government except that offered by the polling organization. And many of the great policy errors made by Presidents during this century have been made because of the misreading of election returns, seeing mandates where none exists.

"In one other respect, polls can be important during election periods. Only totals show up on voting machines; it is impossible to discover how young people voted, or persons on welfare, or how conservatives or liberals registered their views. The polls provide such information.

"In sum, polls can supply the data needed to make the

electoral process intelligible; they can shed light on the reasons why citizens vote and the way they vote; they can make the whole process of electing public officials more interesting and meaningful to the average citizen."

* * * *

Now we resume the review of the outside influences that have an impact—or fail to have one—on public opinion. The first—the government (President and Congress) has been surveyed. The second is the media, to which the next chapter is devoted.

Chapter 9
THE PRESS: PRO AND CON

Of the forces that create public opinion the media are ranked second—outweighed only by the Presidency. A free press is a basic ingredient of democracy and throughout the discussions there was endorsement of Jefferson's dictum: "Were it left to me to decide whether we should have a government without newspapers, or newspapers without a government, I should not hesitate a moment to prefer the latter."

The statistics are impressive: some 1,774 daily, 8,900 weekly newspapers; 934 television stations in the country—705 commercial and over 229 noncommercial; 7,500 radio stations—4,393 AM stations, 2,482 commercial FM stations, and 625 noncommercial FM stations.

What are the functions of this powerful communications apparatus? How well does it perform, especially with international news? What are its faults? How can they be corrected? These are all vital questions that require answers if the press is to fulfill its role as a prime factor in improving public opinion.

Special attention was paid to the coverage of foreign news because what is published in the American press has, or can have, a decisive impact on American public opinion. Also the reports sent from the United States and printed abroad can be a prime factor in forming the American image in the rest of the world.

An extensive series of tests, questionnaires, and interviews was made in the effort to clarify these questions. These were the most important surveys:

1. Reports were made by twenty-one correspondents of the Columbia Journalism Review on the performance of the newspapers in several categories, especially interpretation, minority viewpoints, objectivity, and the impact on opinion. The replies provided useful insights into the difficulties of producing an informed opinion.

2. For a period of eight days, students and researchers examined the twenty papers with the largest circulations in the country to determine the quality of their international coverage. The project was concerned especially with the quantity of news and the amount of interpretation.

3. For two weeks the analysts examined six stories in these twenty newspapers in an effort to determine whether the reader was able to get from them an understandable and coherent account of events. The manner of testing the papers was subjective: assuming that Mr. Markel was the news editor for this particular week, he indicated how he would have played the six stories and posed certain questions that in his opinion needed to be answered if these

complex events were to be made understandable to the average reader.

4. Some forty editors of the foreign news were asked to report on what their philosophy of coverage was—why they did not print more, how they gauged the reader interest, and especially what they would recommend in the way of better coverage.

Six Large Questions

These are the six questions to which answers were particularly sought: 1. How much foreign news does the press supply? 2. What is the quality of that news? 3. How much interpretation is there and how valuable is it? 4. Does the news play supply perspective? 5. What is the quality of the writing? 6. Is too much space allotted to trivia?

These are the approximate answers, which represent a consensus based on the surveys.

1. The news space given to reporting of foreign news totals 17% of the whole news allotment, but this is a misleading figure because it includes trivia, features, and so-called human interest stories, which, if deducted, leaves probably not more than 10%. This is obviously inadequate for reporting a world in a revolutionary period and is accounted for by the fact that reader interest in foreign news is rated high by only six of the thirty-seven editors; moderate by twenty-four; and low by seven.

2. As for the quality of the news, there is often a lack of expertness, due to the fact that correspondents are often shifted in order to get "a fresh point of view" and so do not have the feel of the country that a good dispatch reflects. The *New York Times* and *Los Angeles Times* were rated highest for consistent performance and quality of

news. Of the remaining seventeen newspapers, some scored high in interpretation on some stories but very low on others.

3. Interpretation of international news is minimal and, in some newspapers, nonexistent. Instead of interpretation, one is likely to find opinion in the guise of background. Most of the copy is supplied by the wire services and in their effort to be objective they are likely, when they supply interpretation, to do it as separate pieces rather than incorporating it in the main story.

4. According to the findings about the six top stories, the reader does not acquire perspective on the news. For example, the results of the eight-day survey indicated that none of the twenty newspapers gave front-page display consistently to as many as three of the designated news stories each day. Three of those six major stories could not be included in this part of the survey because of scant or nonexistent coverage in most of the papers. The *New York Times, Los Angeles Times,* and *Washington Post* averaged between two and three stories a day; eleven papers averaged between one and two; and ten averaged one or none a day.

5. As for literary quality, in the case of foreign reportage the aim should be clarity and accuracy. Too often a virtually unqualified statement in the first paragraph will be qualified in a statement in the sixth paragraph.

6. Because of their belief that the reader is not interested in foreign news, many editors are likely, when they print reports from abroad, to play up the sensational rather than the important news. As a result, explanation is crowded out by trivia.

On the whole the surveys indicate that American newspapers are lax in their coverage of international news. The majority provide little more than the bare essentials, not enough to provide any clear view of what is going on in the rest of the world.

Study of TV News

We undertook a week-long survey of nightly television network news broadcasts to determine the amount of foreign news, of interpretation, of understandability, and of objectivity. The amount of foreign news was found to be exceedingly low on all three networks; interpretation was virtually absent; objectivity, which is exceedingly difficult to measure in coverage as brief as television provides, was rated as adequate, so far as the presentation was concerned.

But there is another measure of objectivity. Because of the limits of time, only a few angles of complex stories can be covered in single telecasts; consequently, the decision as to which facts are to be included and which omitted sometimes leads to distortion. Certain important stories were discovered not to have been covered at all, perhaps because they were lacking in visual impact, or perhaps because they had long-range rather than immediate importance.

Overall comment made by the observers was that television coverage is too scattered and not intensive enough. The inclusion of at least fifteen to twenty stories may make the viewer aware of important events, but if he is interested, he can probably gain real knowledge of these happenings only through reading newspapers or periodicals. Coverage was generally found to be quite superficial, bland, and unimaginative. National news completely overshadowed international coverage. Many analysts felt that there was a deliberate avoidance of interpretation in order to achieve a low-keyed, unbiased image.

Television's nightly network news broadcasts present the news in rapid-fire order. Explanation and connecting material are needed but are rarely supplied. When time is taken out for commercials, twenty-one minutes or so remain for news coverage. Generally, at the end of each broadcast, when a relatively longer story is attempted, it is in the form of a feature, and it is likely to be light in theme.

The news programs were extended to a half hour from fifteen minutes several years ago, but the extra fifteen minutes have been given over to features rather than to news. Only the documentaries supply interpretation, but they are infrequent. Some network executives defend the way the news is presented, explaining that the network news programs are headline services that inform people in a concise manner of the major news events of the day; they cannot and do not perform the same service as newspapers because of time limitations and because of the nature of the medium. They also point out that since networks operate under the licensing requirements of the Federal Communications Commission, news analysis can be a more difficult area for television than for newspapers, which are not licensed.

The Press Indicted

These findings reinforce other counts in the indictment of the press. Critics of the newspapers and television news broadcasts charge that they fail to supply the essential facts accurately or in perspective; that they barrage the public with a welter of unrelated news stories; that they fail to separate the significant from the trivial, and, much too often, neglect the minority viewpoint. Elements of the press are condemned for concentrating on the sensational—scandal, gossip, and lurid crimes. In general, the view was expressed that the media fail to show that international news is relevant to the lives of readers and viewers at a time when actions by the federal government and events in foreign countries may profoundly affect American lives.

A mounting issue is this: Is the press too free in that it publishes material prejudicial to a defendant in a criminal trial? In other words, have the media created a conflict between the First Amendment, which guarantees freedom of the press, and the Sixth Amendment, which provides for fair trial? The issue has been underlined recently by the Persico case, in which, despite warnings of the presiding judge, newspapers printed the prior criminal record and other background material prejudicial to the defendant. In this case the court held that the media had gravely violated the rights of the defendant.

Further charges of media irresponsibility are made in connection with leaks of information; there are times, it is maintained, when certain news must be withheld temporarily for the good of the nation. Watergate obscured the issue because there was confusion between leaks regarding public misdemeanors, which should be known, and leaks involving national security, which obviously should not be. Nearly every official in Washington, it is now alleged, has a favorite journalist to whom he passes information.

These excesses and failures have led to a massive credibility gap between the public and the media. Some editors like to believe that the prime reason for the credibility gap is the tendency of the reader-listener to blame them for the blackness of the news. As in the Middle Ages when kings ordered the beheading of bearers of ill tidings, so the reader-listener psychologically decapitates those who publish unpleasant facts. Observers generally say, however, that while there may be some substance to the argument, there are more solid reasons for the mistrust—the inaccuracies, the shoddy coverage, the disregard for the public interest in the search for scoops, and the like—in short, a confusion of liberty with license, freedom with free-booting.

To Regain Credibility

Finally there came the basic query: What can the press do to regain credibility? Of the many answers, these are the most urgent: it must pledge itself to responsibility as compensation for freedom; it must look upon itself as a semi-public institution with a corresponding obligation; it must rate as its first objective the news assignment—information and its meaning—rather than accenting entertainment and features. Integrity, dedication, education—these are the three benchmarks of the worthy press.

The first axiom, it was suggested, might be this: There are times when it is more important to serve the national interest than to obtain an exclusive story.

Likewise, the Bill of Rights, it is asserted, must be scrupulously observed. At one point in the Watergate trials it was suggested that, regardless of the rightness of the verdict, there were episodes that might well have been characterized as trial by newspaper.

"Accuracy, terseness, accuracy" was the Pulitzer slogan. It is still valid, the more so since the credibility gap developed. Corrections, it was emphasized, must be made fully and prominently and not hidden among the unclassified advertising.

Various other measures were advocated. Mr. Reedy said that the problem is one of a lack of diversity. "There are things that can be done about it, reasonable and within the resources at our command. First, various monopolistic influences are forcing newspapers to operate with obsolete, uneconomic equipment. When I went to South America a few years ago I discovered that almost every newspaper was about fifty years ahead of American newspapers in equipment that cuts the mechanical costs and thereby permits more resources for the editorial side of the paper. If we were using such equipment in the United States, then we would be much freer and would have not only greater ability to improve the editorial content but also a chance of bringing about more competition."

More Than Money

Mr. Markel raised the question of whether, if newspapers were in better economic shape, they would do a better job. This exchange took place.

Mr. Reedy said, "A newspaper can dominate a certain market and unfortunately it will survive and prosper regardless, because it carries certain types of information that are not news—the supermarket ads, the drugstore ads, the beer ads. It is entirely possible for a newspaper to make money though it may offer the readers very little in the way of news."

Mr. Markel remarked: "That's why your thesis is wrong. They have the money and they don't improve their product." Mr. Reedy was unperturbed: "I am very, very skeptical of persuading people to make positive efforts for improvement when they make money without it. I am convinced that unless you get to this question of competition you are not going to resolve the problem."

There was agreement, however, that "what a free press means is that a publisher can do what he wants to do, that he can perform as well or as badly as he elects."

The panel then considered the impact of the press. The first conclusion was that the news has much greater influence than the editorials. Doubt was expressed that more than twenty percent of the readers read the editorial page; moreover, the columnist to a large extent has taken the place of the home-bred editorial writer.

Finally, Mr. Markel expressed his opinion of the status of the press. "I have always said that if there are bad newspapers it is because there are bad readers and because so many editors are content—more than that, eager—to give the reader what he wants instead of trying to educate him to want the right news. This all sounds pretty idealistic; but keep in mind that the old system did not work, and led only to credibility gaps."

Interpretation an Issue

A spirited debate took place over "interpretation." Mr. Markel took a strong position on the absolute need of background and explanation. Setting down facts without giving their meaning is practically useless, he said. Without background material the reader or viewer cannot be expected to arrive at reasoned conclusions about such subjects as détente, inflation, or the energy crisis. News, he insisted, means more than factual coverage; it includes both the recording and appraisal of trends. Mere reports are no longer adequate in these days of complex events.

Interpretation he defined as "an objective judgment based on knowledge and appraisal of a situation—good information and sound analysis; it reveals the deeper sense of the news, providing setting, sequence, and above all, significance. It is an indispensable ingredient in the reporting of national and international news." Interpretation, he stressed, is not opinion, which is a subjective judgment that should be confined to the editorial pages and labeled as such.

This endorsement of interpretation produced a raft of controversy. The opposition contended that to ensure objectivity news reports must be confined to facts; if interpretation is included, the writer has moved into the area of opinion. Mr. Landrey called for caution:

"We have to be careful when we allow moralists to tell us what we should be revealing about our own country and other countries, from one point of view or another. These people are mostly special pleaders, and I think we can take refuge only in what little objectivity, fairness, and balance we have, letting the chips fall where they may."

Mr. Markel pointed out that he was not in any way denigrating the ideal of objectivity. Despite the difficulty of achieving it, objectivity must be one of the chief endeavors of journalism. Nevertheless, interpretation should and can be as objective as factual reporting.

Mr. von Krusenstiern argued that the reporter has to be more than a tape recorder. "News reports should be written by people who not only can tell what occurred yesterday but who can provide the background to explain why it occurred. And the interpretation should be on the news pages, not on the editorial page.

"For years Americans, living in splendid isolation, didn't require too much information about the rest of the world, but today all that has changed. Events that occur in far-off parts of the world affect Americans quite directly. Now the media have to inform people about what is going on everywhere, and interpretation is vital. Such explanation does not involve any partisan political approach, hence the argument that interpretation entails opinion is not a valid one."

Mr. O'Neill also argued in favor of interpretation. "The definition of news should be broadened," he said, "to include nonphysical happenings. During the 1950s the migration of blacks from the rural south to the northern cities was going on. This was not a news event, but a profound thing was happening, and the country was surprised by the result. There are many things going on which do not fit the traditional definition of news. For example, in 1965 the government cut back on research and development and it is now having profound effects."

Interpretation, the majority held, is indispensable if the complex news of these revolutionary days is to be understood.

* * * *

To the President and media as the first and second of the outside forces that influence public opinion, there must be added education in all its forms and at almost all ages. Vital in the process is a free and untainted flow of information, as demonstrated in the next chapter.

Chapter 10
INFORMATION IS VITAL

One dictum was stated and restated in the course of the discussions: There must be good information; the public must absorb it and act upon it; otherwise, the democratic process will be stalled.

The information question was debated at length. Mr. Markel opened the discussion with this statement: "The majority of the electorate is uninformed or misinformed; in any case, not sufficiently informed to meet the needs of the day. The voters do not turn out in impressive numbers; the issues are not well understood; in the '72 election there was virtually no debate over these questions—only emotion, most of it negative. But the issues were there, nevertheless, and remain."

There was an immediate challenge from Mr. Reedy, who said, "We make a fetish out of this information business.

There is enough information available for the task if it is utilized by the political forces. You can pump out information until the cows come home, but it is not going to make any difference. What does make the difference are the attitudes of people and their determination to do something. But that, in turn, requires political maturity. We have new forces but they are still politically immature; once they are politically mature, they will be able to get all the information they need.

"Generally speaking, tremendous amounts of information are more confusing than they are clarifying. My heart bleeds for the future historians trying to assess what actually happened in the last ten or fifteen years. Their problem is not that there will be a lack of information, but rather that there will be so much information that no living human being, even an Aristotle, a Bertrand Russell, a St. Thomas, or a St. Augustine, could possibly digest it.

"This is fundamentally a political problem—the need of finding a base upon which new movements can stand. We are in an era of shifting political constituencies that are in need not of information but of sophistication. They do not know how to handle themselves; they haven't found leaders; they don't understand coalition politics.

"When Roosevelt worked out the coalition that led to the epoch-making election of 1932, there was no problem of feeding out information. That coalition had been in formation for a number of years. The Democratic convention of 1924 had been a complete fiasco; the Democratic convention of 1928 could not find a leader to speak for it; but by 1972 the Democrats had found a leader and the convention had learned how to act. People have to learn how to act politically.

"One of the great myths of all time and one of the things

that makes a President so formidable is the saying, 'If you only knew what the President knows.' Well, the truth is, what you don't know that the President does know is that he had dinner with an old crony the night before, or that he has had a visit from a boyhood friend who happened to have had a contract in selling shoes in Southeast Asia. Nothing of more consequence.

"This question of information is greatly exaggerated. The idea that there is an arcane body of knowledge that is denied to the people is utterly false. The President makes up his mind on just about the same information as you have. The difference is that he has immediately, at his fingertips, a tremendous machine, which starts gathering information to reinforce his opinion. These things are questions of political judgment, and in terms of political judgment, information is quite secondary."

The Secrecy Debate
Mr. Reedy was asked, did this mean there is little need for classifying information? "There is a tremendous body of classified information, and what does it amount to? I have noticed that people emerge from a reading of the Pentagon Papers with precisely the opinions they had before they read them. I do not think the Pentagon Papers add much in the way of history. They are fascinating because of the light they shed on the workings of government, because they reveal that there was a tremendous debate going on in the Pentagon, which nobody outside of the government—and very few people within the government—knew about.

"I repeat: We make too much of a fetish of information. One of the worst things that's happened to us is that we abolished the Delphic Oracle. This was a terribly useful institution. When you went to the Oracle, it gave you an answer that made you think. When the Persians invaded Greece, the Athenians went to the Oracle and the Oracle told them: 'Thou shalt defend Athens behind a wall—behind a wooden wall.' That was a marvelous answer, because the Athenians had to figure out what that wooden wall was, which meant they went back and thought.

"If they had gone to a computer, the computer would have told them, as it told Secretary McNamara, that when the kill ratio reaches eight to one, you will have won the war. Well, the kill ratio reached eight to one, and the war went on. Obviously the computer had failed; the difficulty is that the computer gives you back only what you put into it. It is given back in a way that makes you think it's a real answer, but it is not a real answer; it is only a mathematical computation.

"The most useful thing we could do is to go back to Delphic Oracles so people will start thinking again."

There was general disagreement with Mr. Reedy's viewpoint, a feeling that there was much concealment by government. There is a constant complaint that the Executive does not make enough information about foreign affairs available either to the Congress or to the people. Obviously in diplomacy everything cannot be put upon the table and everything cannot be made public, but there is no doubt among those who know in the State Department that there is overclassification and a tendency among career officers to play it safe by giving out as little as possible.

For Security? Maybe

The Executive contends that classification and censorship are purely for security reasons. But it is generally agreed that there is overclassification and certainly there are outstanding examples, especially in connection with the Vietnam war, in which information was withheld and in some cases false information given out.

Mr. Lewis sounds an alarm: "People don't realize to what an extent decisions of very fundamental character are made in secret. It isn't just the classification system of confidential, or secret, or top secret, but now there are superclassifications, in which even the names of the classification are not known. The idea of secrecy is pervasive in the government and I don't think you can have public participation or indeed an adequate check on the floor of the Congress."

Thus material essential to understanding is kept from the Congress and hence from the people through the media, upon which devolves the task of ferreting out stories that are, but should not be classified. There is no doubt that the whole classification system needs revision, but that is no easy job, because one development may affect several different departments and the safest course for any official is to use his stamp rather than his head.

An outstanding example of secrecy was the decision to bomb Cambodia, which became one of the items in the talk of impeachment. There were constant denials of the fact, but it was a fact and it was certain to come out in the news before too long.

"Executive privilege"—a provision by which certain of the White House staff can refuse to testify without giving any reason for the refusal—has also been used to keep information from the public; the President has refused to divulge information or to give out documents to the Congress on the ground that this would be a violation of executive right.

Mr. Reedy was asked whether he would make public

the proceedings of a Security Council meeting—supposedly a highly classified affair—as Jack Anderson did. He replied, "I have sat in on an awful lot of Security Council meetings. I think if you printed the transcripts of these meetings verbatim and chiseled them on Mount Rushmore in letters six feet high, the Russians would have learned no more than they already know.

"I am reminded of a very wonderful line from Bolitho: In *Twelve Against the Gods* he describes an elaborate ritual to keep a bit of information from the public and he concludes: 'The secret was that there was no secret.' And that's exactly what is happening with an awful lot of this stuff. I think there are no secrets."

Mr. Hyman remarked that "the real question is—how much of the whole truth and nothing but the truth do you reveal and at what time? I can imagine that there are circumstances when you wouldn't want to tell the whole truth, no more than a doctor tells the patient the whole truth. But there is a legitimacy of timing in such things.

"The question is how much you reveal at the outset of action and how much you reveal after action has been taken, so that the public itself can exercise its one great controlling power, which is the power to praise or to censure. I cannot see how the public can design a policy; this has to come out of the leadership institution. But the public can reward and punish and it can do this only if it knows who did what, when and why."

This problem of secrecy—and deceit, censorship, classification, misleading reports, trial balloons—has become a fundamental issue, and logically so, because again it is said that an informed opinion depends on two essential actions; the information must be made available and the public must absorb and act upon it. Both ingredients are now missing; both must be supplied; one without the other is of no value.

* * * *

What are the remedies for these large gaps—in information and in the use of it? Education is the simple and only answer. That is the theme of the next two chapters.

Chapter 11
THE PRIMARY STEP

The people must be persuaded to demand that their representatives in the executive and legislative offices and in the press provide an ample supply of information and then the people must act upon it. What is involved is a broad campaign of education in which all the forces competent to influence public opinion take part.

Mr. Katzenbach puts the issue this way: "How can our foreign policy gain that public consensus without which no foreign policy can hope to succeed? Our foreign policy must be based on factual premises that are accepted by the overwhelming majority of the American people. This means that the President must reestablish the credibility of that office; that there must be broad support in the Congress and in the press and public for the policy he seeks to for-

ward, and virtually total confidence that there is no manip-
ulation of facts to prove the wisdom of that policy or,
which may often be the same thing, the honest commitment of his administration to it.

"We may have to modify or abandon foreign policy objectives supported by many to arrive at a satisfactory level
of public confidence. But until an administration can
achieve it, we cannot hope to succeed in any foreign policy, however modest it may be."

Education—the ability to discover, to understand, and to
absorb—is needed, from the primary schools onward. "The
problem," Mr. Hyman said, "is not what you do with the
mass of people but with the intermediate leaders. I have
always been struck by the biblical story of God's promise
to Abraham: 'If you could find ten good men in the city
of Sodom, you would save the city.' In my early days, I
used to wonder why the number was ten and, as I grew
older, I realized that if you find ten good men in a city,
they will save it themselves without divine intervention.

"So the problem in education is this: How do you produce ten good people in each community? In an effort to
meet that problem, the University of Chicago has set up
public affairs programs which are quite different from the
usual how-to-do-it courses.

"For three years, a group of young people brings to bear
on a single issue a multiplicity of disciplines involved in
that issue. We are planning to send into the various communities graduates who are broad-gauged and able to tackle community problems in contrast with the narrow voca-
tional-oriented specialists. Obviously you cannot tell before
ten years elapse what will emerge out of these experiments.
But at least there is the hope that something different can
be achieved."

Is Education Amiss?

Dr. Fatemi attacked the basic system of education: "Our colleges and universities suffer from the same problems that confront the government. In the government I discern neither national planning nor national purpose, and the same broad objectives are missing in our educational institutions.

"Education should have two purposes: It should bring about understanding of the large problems that confront us rather than producing semiliterate citizens; and it must provide for the training of good citizens who know their duty and recognize their responsibility to their country and to the rest of the world.

"Moreover, our system of education should provide for the training of leaders. We should recognize the responsibility of the educators, of the universities that produced the 'best and the brightest' in the Kennedy administration and also the plumbers and the lawyers in Nixon's administration. These university-trained men are dealing with the complicated questions of today, but their training is of 1936 and '37, and most of them never took a course in what this world is about. Our universities must be brought up to date in order to train people for the next thirty or forty years.

"We have to prepare people for professions, but universities must teach their students that they are first of all citizens, then medical doctors and businessmen, and that as citizens in a democracy they must know what is going on in the country. They must be concerned. If I were the president of the university, the day that the freshmen arrived I would tell them, 'Pay four years of your tuition. Now, whoever wants to get a diploma and nothing more, here is your diploma; get out. And those of you who want to study, stay here and we will give you a proper education.' "

Only if these educational forces move determinedly and unitedly toward the goal will public opinion achieve a place that will give foreign policy the solid base it requires. As Professor Reischauer eloquently put it: "Before long, humanity will face many grave difficulties that can only be solved on a global scale. Education is not moving rapidly enough in the right direction to produce the knowledge about the outside world and the attitudes toward other people that may be essential for human survival within a generation or two. This, I feel, is a much greater international problem than the military balance of power that absorbs so much of our attention today."

PART IV:
DEMOCRACY TESTED

The problems we face in our search for a new world role have been explored and profiles of leaders and people presented. In the course of the discussion, some doubt was expressed about the efficacy of democracy. To clarify their doubts, light was sought on the nation's attitudes and difficulties. The issues involved are discussed in the following chapters.

Chapter 12
PARAMOUNT PROBLEMS

So you have the ignorance and lethargy of the public abetted by the secrecy of the government. And this at a time of international crisis and a baffling series of problems at home. Without information and concern, solutions cannot be found for either. The domestic issues are just as complex as the foreign issues; as has been demonstrated, they are parts of a whole. So the panel was asked to survey the full gamut of problems. Mr. Reedy led off:

"The number-one overriding problem is the adjustment of the political structure to the new social forms that have been emerging with great speed, including the questions asked by the women, the young people, and the other groups who are now finding voices. Possibly this paramount issue arises out of the fact that for the first time in history man has been separated from the production process; there is no longer a place for totally unskilled people to go.

"The number-two problem is the adjustment of the economy to the basic fact that we are overspent and overextended. We have been living off credit for the last ten, fifteen, twenty years. Eventually we have to face up to this problem of credit.

"A third problem concerns the adjustment of our perceptions to the issues arising out of the fact that large masses of poor people have been excluded from the development of society. This is the real relief problem.

"The fourth problem is somewhat similar, namely, the adjustment of the economy to the fact that skilled people are becoming surplus so rapidly—the sort of thing that is happening on the West Coast where Ph.D.'s who were making 25–30,000 dollars a year a few months ago are now driving taxi cabs and looking for welfare stamps.

"The final problem is the need to discover some absolute values for our young people who are emerging into a world where there are no such values. There goes on among the young a desperate search for what in the old theological days we would have called their souls. (It is no longer fashionable to use the word *soul,* but I think it does denote something basic.) "

Miss Friedan said she would put first "the need for purposes in life, something beyond sheer material accumulation. Along with this, there is the problem of propping up the pockets of poverty so that everyone gets his share of the material things. Second, a way must be found for people to participate in the decision-making process, in government, in corporations, and in other institutions. This would serve to bridge differences among the various political factions.

"Third, there is a huge problem of war and peace. There must be a psychological desensitization of people to war;

somehow we must learn that these carnage circuses are not needed to keep us occupied and to keep the economy going. I believe we could almost do without a defense department.

"Fourth is the problem of leisure. Increasing numbers of people are going to live longer and longer lives, to have second and even third adolescences. This will result in changes in the whole time structure in people's lives and the methods of education.

"Finally, there is the women's revolution. The women's movement will finish its agenda and become part of the decision-making process and move into the main stream of action. This will bring about revolutionary changes in the family, in child care, in city planning, and so forth. Moreover, women will be coming in increasing numbers into government and, in all likelihood, will shift the political agenda to the human side, to human priorities and human problems. And I hope that out of it all will evolve a new human politics."

The Old Problems

Mr. Hyman found the issue simpler: "In a way the problems that confront us in the next four years are the old problems of government. There is no mystery about them; they are stated in the Preamble to the Constitution —the problems of union, justice, domestic tranquillity, happiness, and the rest of it.

"The problems of today are specific manifestations of these old problems; they are, in fact, the eternal problems of government. One of the great tensions is the tension on all our government institutions. We went through a presidential campaign in 1972 and the central issue was the Presidency itself. Yet there were no speeches about the

Presidency, the one institution through which all the solutions to these problems are presumably going to funnel. We must take a look at the institutional structure of the Congress and the Presidency.

"Again, we have to take a look at the whole business of bigness and littleness. This is a theme that runs through everything—big cities, little cities, big universities, little universities, big families, little families, big government, little government, and so forth.

"This leads back to the problem of how the instruments of power ought to be controlled. And this, in turn, leads to the issue that cuts through almost everything, namely the minority-majority relationship. Question: Does 50% plus a fraction of 1% make a political or legal right? What kind of rights do you give to the 49% less a fraction of 1%? How is the relationship to be adjusted?

"More specifically, we are confronted with the problem of a professional army. This is a fundamental constitutional question and it can prove almost fatal unless we change the character of the military profession and its impact on civilian life.

"Among the other initial questions is the problem of time and leisure. Then there is the issue of the criminal justice system. We are spending billions of dollars on criminal justice; we are setting up programs on criminal justice in many of the universities; yet what we are doing is injecting into the system a lot of police-trained people with none of the breadth that the task requires."

Professor Fatemi said that the first question in his mind was the "re-humanizing of our society." He explained: "We must rededicate ourselves, both leaders and followers, to honesty, to truthfulness, to one another, to tell things as they are.

"The second problem is the crisis in our educational system. Our universities are in the tradition of the nineteenth century and the period before World War II; they do not produce men and women capable of facing a new world. We have a second-rate educational system for a first-rate nation.

"The third problem is that of learning the practice of restraint of power both at home and abroad, recognizing that we are facing a new world in which we have a large role to play but that we cannot fulfill that role if we waste our energies and act without responsibility, as we have been doing in the last twenty-five years.

"Another vital question concerns American economics, domestically and internationally. We are bankrupt internationally; by that I mean the dollar does not have the worth of other currencies like the mark and the franc, and if we continue to spend money abroad as we are doing now, not only shall we have a devaluation of the dollar but also a collapse of the whole international system which we have done so much to establish in the last many years.

"Finally, there is the problem of full participation in our great democracy—a problem that arises either from the failure of leadership or of the people. We must return to the tradition of trust in the people, looking upon them as partners in a great enterprise in which all must work together. There is no one who knows everything and there are no masters. In short, we must return to government of the people, by the people, and for the people."

Forces of Change

Dr. Gallup said, "I see, as one of the big issues of the next few years, the question of race, and the issues allied to that—such as crime and welfare. Another grave problem is the question of the continuation of price and wage controls. One of the biggest issues before the country is the court system and, allied with it, the prison system."

Dr. Gallup was asked whether he thought relations with the communists presented a problem. He replied: "I do not think that is likely. I do not believe the question will bother people the way it did in the past, certainly not in the way it did in the early fifties."

Dr. Lazarsfeld added: "I agree with the points made by George Gallup, but I would add two more. I think the question of conglomerates, or large organizations, will play a considerable role in the future because either we accept the fact that the country will be run by large business organizations or we have to do something about it. But now the situation is confused; on the one hand there are those large corporations which become more and more powerful, and on the other, we still have the terminology of free enterprise and competition.

"Second, above and beyond the issue of defense spending, there is the question of the role of the military; there is the issue of a volunteer army, and the question of whether it will be a black army—because the unemployment rate of blacks is so high."

In addition to specific problems, some of the underlying causes were described. For example, Mr. Semple said that "a national argument goes on between those who defend and those who deplore the works and values of a generation—a division between factions favoring and opposed to change that is sharper than the division between Republicans and Democrats, or between liberals and conservatives.

"The forces of change are led by the young and by the poor; they ascribe social injustice and deterioration to the unfair distribution of power. The rest of the citizenry, though not without grievances and frustrations, regards the American system as basically sound and capable of self-improvement and tends to fear the remedies of the rebels more than any ailment. From these distinct perceptions emerge contrasting positions on current problems."

Mr. Reedy summed up the debate: "Our major problem at the moment is that we are in a state of transition. Old political forces are failing but they are still very strong; new political forces are getting stronger. But the people do not have a clear-cut understanding of the predominant political forces. These forces must have time to adjust, to discover how to work together, to build a new grand coalition, such as the one constructed by Roosevelt, but which no longer exists. This cannot be done by blueprint, but by leaders who arise the way the prophets arose."

*   *   *   *

In the light of these problems, what is the future of democracy? Is there a better form of government that would facilitate the solutions? The answers, necessarily speculative, are given in the next chapter.

Chapter 13
"WORST"? — "BEST"

The series of tragedies that have beset us in the past five years—Vietnam, Watergate, the recession, the international tangle—has raised questions about the form and performance of the government and doubts about democracy itself. Are these doubts valid?

Before discussion, a reprise: The facts are that the nation is not well informed and that public opinion, on which democracy ultimately depends, is rudderless. The voters do not turn out in impressive numbers. The issues are not well understood; in the 1972 election there was little debate over issues, only emotion, most of it negative, even though there were important issues involved. There is indicated, therefore, a large job of information and education to be done, by the President and the other political leaders, by the formal educators, and by the media.

As for the primary question about democracy, Churchill provided the answer: "Democracy is the worst form of government in the world except anything else that anybody has ever thought of." Mr. MacEachron quoted it and went on to say: "That applies to our situation in the United States. We are probably worse off than we'd like to be, but we are better off, I think, on the whole, than most countries in the world. It is important to recognize that.

"Part of the problem is that we are very hard on ourselves and aware of our own deficiencies. Yet I would say by most measures ours is still the most powerful nation in the world, and that gives us a special international role. Although we are doing pretty well as a people, we are in a race to educate ourselves and develop our institutions and so on, so that we can cope with a world that is exceedingly complicated but also very exciting and very challenging. I think if we are wise we can be very hopeful."

Certain opinion leaders have been inclined to play down the majority and concentrate their efforts on the informed "elite." Walter Lippmann, for example, advocated "intelligence bureaus" (staff experts) to provide "illumination" for the decision-makers. "The purpose," he said, "is not to burden every citizen with expert opinions on all questions, but to push that burden away from him toward the responsible administrators."

Gabriel Almond, Jr., has also questioned the classical democratic theory: "The democratic myth is that the people are inherently wise and just and that they are the real rulers of the republic. There are inherent limitations in modern society in the capacity of the public to understand the issues. The function of the public in a democratic policy-making process is to set certain policy criteria in the form of widely held values and expressions. The policies themselves, however, are the products of leadership groups ("elites"). In view of these considerations many of the moralistic exhortations to the public to inform itself and to play an active role in policy-making have the virtues and failings of evangelism."

A Contrary View

To these views, this was the answer: the Lippmann formula is almost the negation of democracy: its advocates concede that we should have a government "of" and "for" the people, but they feel that government "by" the people is almost unattainable. What is missing in their calculations is this factor: The ultimate decision, the decision as to who the decision-makers shall be, is made by the voter. Moreover, the "elite," contemplating the world from their "navel observatories," or the experts closeted with their computers, or the chosen ones in their seats of power are as divided in their viewpoints as the men in the street. Obviously it is a long pull to achieve an informed majority, but that is the ultimate hope. Immediately, the goal is to increase the size of the informed minority.

One of the grave charges of recent years has been that the government was moving toward a kind of totalitarianism and that the First Amendment was being eroded. If this were true, democracy would suffer a fatal blow. The statement was unanimously held false by the panel.

Fascism? No Danger

Mr. Hyman protested. "I am weary," he said, "of hearing all this talk about Fascism. I think it is a playing with words. What is Fascism? Take a look at the title of the Nazi Party—National Socialist Workers' Party. Can you

imagine a Republican President talking about a National
Socialist Workers' Party? As for Fascism, it is a bastard
Socialism. And until a President starts talking about bastard Socialism and workers, I will not start worrying. You
may have straight-out police action but not Fascism. I
think we ought to use words precisely."

Mr. Reedy disagreed: "I see the First Amendment under very, very heavy attack. I really don't believe this has
been just a question of the Nixon Administration, although
I think his administration accelerated the process. This
process set in before, and it is somewhat independent of
the normal forms of politics. There are so many factors
involved here that it is a very difficult subject to cover in
a single answer.

"Differentiation must be made between the printed and
the electronic media, for two reasons. First, the printed
press does not have to face the fear of licensing, and second, it has a long tradition. (You can trace the printed
press back at least 200 years.) The electronic media, on
the other hand, suffer from the fact that they are licensed.

"I think there is a grave question as to whether
the media would stand up and fight if that licensing power
were used to crack down on them. People operating under
a license are always operating under fear, and they are
likely to back down more quickly before governmental attacks. Nor do the electronic media have a full-grown tradition yet, and tradition is terribly important in a situation
like this. People with tradition are more likely to stand up
than people without it.

"The overall thing that is happening is that as our society becomes more and more interdependent, as it becomes more massive in terms of numbers and more delicate in terms of balances, there develops a greater ten-

dency for the government to become remote and aloof, and a greater tendency for people at the top to ask: 'Why should some element of our society be independent and refuse to cooperate with us in doing the things that we want done in order to make society better?'

"This is really what is eroding the First Amendment. It is not so much a question of law, which can only effect certain shifts in the wording. Even if you revise the First Amendment, I think there would be great difficulty in suppressing the press through straight-out application of the law. It is the indirect pressures that are the danger: the constant attacks and the increasing dependence of huge commercial institutions on governmental action."

The Real Danger

Mr. Reedy was asked if there had not been direct attacks on freedom of the press in recent years by the government. He replied: "In the case of the Pentagon Papers an effort was made to establish prepublication censorship. The effort failed, but I don't like the way it failed. I am concerned when I read those Supreme Court decisions, but the case is still open. The reason the Pentagon Papers case received so much attention is because it is recent and because it is the only instance like it in all our history as a nation. To find anything similar you've got to go back to Peter Zenger or even to England. The case of Ellsberg was very, very tricky. It did not involve the press per se; it involved Ellsberg and whether he committed an offense against certain statutes.

"None of this is where the real danger lies. The real danger lies in the growing belief that there should be some way of telling the press to tell the truth, as if anybody knew THE truth. The fact is that the press is becoming more vulnerable, and, if politicians see vulnerability, they will step in."

The British Way

In the background of all these discussions was the question as to whether democracy, as we have it, is really working. The suggestion was made that possibly we should adopt something like the British system—the no-confidence vote, for example.

Mr. Reedy pointed out that "you can't have a no-confidence vote for the simple reason that we have a Presidential, not a parliamentary system under which the chief executive is elected out of the parliament itself.

"I was once very attracted by the concept of the British parliamentary system. I have now discarded it completely. You can have a no-confidence vote only when you have over the chief executive a chief of state, a king or a queen who is immune from temporary transitions. Then it is a very simple matter to make the transfer from one head of government to another. As for the impeachment power, it was never intended to effect a transition, but solely to apply to high crimes and misdemeanors.

"The people of England do not really vote for Churchill or Atlee, or Wilson or the rest. They vote for a parliament and the parliament selects the prime minister. The system will not work unless the legislators choose the chief executive and have the power of recalling him."

Professor Hyman agreed: "It is very difficult to graft on the American system of government any features of the British—as difficult as grafting on the British system any features of the American without changing the whole political complex. These are, in theory at least, two entirely different formulas for responsible government."

Mr. Reedy cited history: "The English parliamentary system began in the thirteenth century in a period when catastrophic mistakes did not occur. Moreover, the British have had six hundred years in which to work things out.

"What we forget is that no governmental system will work unless it is accompanied by a compatible political system. Now you can legislate a governmental system, but you cannot legislate a political system. The British parliamentary system works because British practices of party responsibility give it stability.

"In 1875 the French, after the Franco-Prussian War, wrote a constitution patterned very closely on the British model. They eliminated a king and put in a president. But because they were grafting an alien system on a nation with a different history and different traditions, the French began to have revolving prime ministers. It took nearly a hundred years for them to make their constitution only reasonably workable.

"When you elect a president under a parliamentary system, you elect him for six or twelve years—in any case, an extraordinarily long period of time. The only workable system is one in which the chief executive is a prime minister who is a creature of the parliament. You cannot have both a president and a prime minister; it just doesn't work.

"If we tried the British kind of system in the United States there would be chaos, because we do not have disciplined parties. Of necessity our parties are coalitions. We would be in terrible trouble if we had ideological parties, because we have no way of forming a coalition government. Our chief executive is one man and that is that; his cabinet officers are merely his agents. So we have no way of forming a coalition government. I do not object to the fact that the Republican and Democratic parties are un-ideological; if they were not, our system would collapse.

"I think history has confirmed the statement made by Churchill that democracy has its faults, but of all the systems, democracy is by far the best. That has been demonstrated time and again; it has been demonstrated in the twentieth century when dictatorships of the right have fallen one after another. The dictators tried to make the trains run on time and prescribe ways of life for their subjects, but they have not lasted because man has an unconquerable desire for freedom. The dictatorships of the left have had to modify their policies and will be forced to modify them still further."

Dr. Fatemi added a historic note: "I am reminded of the time when Jefferson and members of his cabinet were discussing the question of what to do about France and England. Jefferson said that a foreign policy made by the government alone could not be the foreign policy of the United States; a permanent policy was one that was debated openly and then supported by the people. For a policy to be lasting, the people of the nation must know about it, and the Congress must accept it."

The discussion ended with a personal declaration by Mr. Markel: "This, then, is the paramount argument: We are pledged to democracy, to government 'of, by, and for the people'; but democracy will not truly work unless its citizens take part in the process.

"Public opinion lags at a time when its relevance and its urgency cannot be overestimated. The task is to make the people aware; never was it so true that if the bell tolls for one it tolls for all.

"But there is no need for pessimism. I, for one, am wholly optimistic—first, because democracy is still the best system devised by man; second, because knowing that in the past we have always somehow muddled through, I am confident that we shall see it through time and again, provided that national interest is put above self-interest and that calm is substituted for blind fear."

PART V:
CONCLUSION AND
COMMENTARY

These final chapters present a summing-up of the conclusions drawn by the editors from the research and the discussions in the panel and classroom sessions. The arrangement of the conclusion is this: first, the findings; second, the larger questions raised in the debates; third, the proposed solutions.

(Note: In the Appendix, there will be found the full text of the questionnaires and the answers to which reference is made in the text.)

CONCLUSION
by Lester Markel

The editors, having reviewed the various surveys and arguments, are convinced that we must revise our foreign policy radically because of the revolutionary changes on the world scene, but we can achieve a successful policy only if we have sound leadership and an informed opinion to support it. Confronted with a tangle of complex problems and a public opinion that is scant and lethargic, the future is uncertain. Heroic measures are needed if we are to succeed in our mission.

For thirty years ours was a place of undisputed supremacy among the nations. Now other powers have risen to challenge our leadership. That does not mean that we shall no longer hold first place, but it does require a complete change in attitude; we must endeavor to substitute cooperation for competition and consultation for diktats. Neither Wilson's premature idealism nor Dulles's power plays will any longer serve our purpose.

For years we nurtured certain illusions; some we have abandoned, but some still plague us. For long periods we had visions of peace and prosperity in isolation and self-sufficiency. But now, except for a small minority, we realize that in this one world we are dependent on others, just as they are dependent on us. But we still cling to other fallacies. For example, we have the idea that we should be loved because we have given freely; we do not realize that nations are like people when it comes to charity; they resent both the gift and the giver. Again, there is still prevalent the idea that it is possible to divide the world into clear categories—capitalism, communism, socialism, etcetera—and apply the same formula to all included in any one category. No. The world has become much more complex than that.

The search for the new role is no simple task. We are confronted with a multitude of problems, national as well as international. In addition, there is a psychological hurdle: Our images of others are false in many respects, just as are theirs of us, owing to faults in communication that there is little effort to correct.

The international problems are of two kinds: those that involve single countries or specific areas, such as a détente with Russia or a settlement in the Near East; and those that are worldwide in scope.

The negotiation with Russia is the most urgent immediate issue, but in the long run the real global crisis is the future of the Third World, that two-thirds of the globe where poverty, overpopulation, pollution, and prejudice exist in monstrous proportions.

The national problems call for a change in attitudes, political and social, and for an end to politics. The development of a sound public opinion—or even one that is reasonably informed—was held vital by the panelists without exception, despite the difficulty of bringing it about. Dean Rusk put it thus:

"In our democracy, a President cannot pursue for very long a major policy without the understanding and support of the American people and of the Congress. At the end of the day the people decide. When one thinks of the peace of reconciliation we made with Germany and Japan, the Marshall Plan, Point Four, the rebuilding of our defense forces after the demobilization following World War II, changing public attitudes on Vietnam, or the pursuit of détente, one must recognize the crucial importance of public opinion."

The Large Questions

Out of the conclusions come certain questions that require answers if we are to achieve that new policy—questions such as these:

● Are we ready to make sacrifices for the national and international good? How much are we willing to do by way of helping the almost helpless Third World? What can we do to change our world image?

● What hope is there of reaching an accord with Moscow? Can we trust the Russians? Is our diplomacy effective in dealing with them?

● What should be the basic elements of a new foreign policy? How much, if any, of the old type of police duty will we undertake? How much cooperation will we have in that effort? Is there any hope for the U.N.?

● What is the prospect for developing leadership in Washington? What do we mean by leadership? How does the President reestablish the credibility of the Presidential office?

• Why do we not have an informed public opinion about foreign affairs? What can be done to bring it about? Is it not essential to democracy?

The answers given by the panelists and researchers to the questions obviously could not be too definite or too complete, because world affairs are in flux and the circumstances change almost from day to day. The answers, however, do clarify the problems requiring prime attention. Here they are:

The Third World

The Third World is the outstanding trouble spot for the future. The balance of nuclear terror has stalemated the cold war in Europe, and the struggle for influence and economic advantage has been shifted to the Third World of the developing nations. The concern is not so much that the Third World will rise against the rich nations in a tremendous class conflict, but that local clashes may draw the superpowers into the struggle. These cold war problems, it is agreed, cannot be handled as moral crusades, but must be approached in a practical way; and the "have nations" must help the "have-not nations," without sentiment and without sermonizing; if they do not, they are likely to be dragged into the quagmire themselves.

The revulsion about the Vietnam war and the expenditure of life and money in that adventure resulted in a trend toward isolation. But such experiences as the oil crisis have made the nation conscious that it cannot go it alone, that this is really an interdependent world.

A change in our image is going to be difficult unless we make every effort not to throw our weight around. The Third World has developed a picture of the United States as a symbol of capitalism and intrigue, and unless we definitely abandon the kind of adventures concocted by the CIA or the sort of intervention practiced in Cambodia, we shall be hard put to it to convince the rest of the world of our good faith.

The Russian Game

A good introduction to the questions raised about Russia is the following observation written by Dean Acheson in 1961: "To our minds international conferences and international negotiations are so completely means for ending conflict that we are blind to the fact that they may be and, in the hands of experts, are equally adapted to continuing it." Acheson believes that we misconceive the role which international meetings play in the Russian strategy of negotiation. The purpose of such meetings to them is not to reach a resolution of a subject or an accommodation. "Negotiation is an act in itself," he explains, "a grandstand play with the world as audience."

The Russians' ultimate objectives are not yet clear, except that they seem to move where it is safe to move and to pull back, as in Cuba, when there is danger of a confrontation. In any case, at the present moment, they are in need of machinery and a number of products, and so they are anxious to arrange trade with us, regardless of ideology. There is no sign that they have given up the Marxist crusade, but they have certainly put it on the shelf for the present in the interest of working out some kind of arrangement with us.

The fear of China also operates as an impetus toward building strength and one of the things they're hoping for is that collaboration with the United States will stimulate their economy and put them in a position to resolve the Chinese problem.

But while the negotiations go on, each nation looks to its military strength. The fact is that, much as we applaud the Bolshoi ballet and the Moscow circus, we do not let down our guard. In brief, there is the possibility of a détente—that is, an armed truce—with Moscow, but little hope of a permanent agreement; so long as free speech and a free press do not exist in Russia, suspicion will not subside.

A New Policy

The question of the essential principles of a new foreign policy involves some definite departures in internal procedures and also a shift in attitudes toward other nations. As for the general changes, Mr. Katzenbach cited a number of radical ones:

"The President needs and wants the support and participation of Congress and the public in formulating his foreign policy."

"The principal makers of foreign-policy decision must be exposed to Congress, the press, and the public."

"We should abandon publicly all cover operations designed to influence political results in foreign countries."

"We must minimize the role of secret information in foreign policy."

"We must reform our classification system and outlook."

"In the present world situation, far greater Congressional and public involvement in formulating our foreign policy seems to me not only right, but nearly inevitable. The most serious problem of a more open foreign policy lies in Congressional response."

"I am prepared to take some losses in our foreign affairs if by so doing we can restore the fundamental of representative democracy to our foreign policy. As Watergate demonstrates, democracy is too fragile to be divided into foreign and domestic affairs. We cannot give the President a free hand in the one without eroding the whole of the government system that all policy seeks to preserve."

This is Arthur Schlesinger's view: "The problem of the reconstruction of our relations with our friends, large and small, will call on rather different skills and different values from those that worked so well in dealing with the great adversary powers. Moreover, the domination of foreign affairs by the White House inexorably tends to place the big deals at a premium and the day-to-day conduct of relations in noncrisis areas at a discount. One must hope that the President will reorganize his management of foreign affairs in a way that will produce intelligent, consistent, and responsible policies—and will do as well for our friends as we have recently done for our enemies."

True Images

There is another defect in the international picture which, if it were corrected, would help greatly to bring about understanding. What is needed is much better and much more accurate communications, a constant effort to improve the flow of the news among nations.

At the present time, the images one nation has of most others are far from accurate. This is due to the fact that the news is sensational or trivial, that such other influences as motion pictures and television give false impressions. One other measure is especially advocated, namely, bipartisanship in foreign policy. This is the way that Secretary Kissinger puts it:

"To appeal for renewed nonpartisan cooperation in foreign policy reflects not a preference but a national necessity. Foreign nations must deal with our Government as an entity, not as a complex of divided institutions. They must be able to count on our maintaining both our national will and our specific undertakings. If they misjudge either, they may be tempted into irresponsibility or grow reluctant to link their destiny to ours. If our divisions lead to a failure of policy, it is the country which will suffer, not one group or one party or one Administration. If our cooperation promotes success, it is the nation which will benefit."

Accuracy of information will bring understanding, and out of understanding it is hoped will come peace.

Leadership

We come then to what has been said about the two top requirements for a sound foreign policy—leadership and public opinion. Leadership, we are convinced, depends on the man himself. Wilson achieved it through his powers of persuasion: Kennedy attained it through his personality; Johnson revealed it in private, but not in public; Truman and Eisenhower won it through Congress. Life at 1600 Pennsylvania Avenue may change a man, but the quality of leadership is inherent and not the product of the environment.

One of the problems that must be solved is the relationship between the President and the Congress. The issue is a hot one, what with the elections coming up next year. There are those who believe that the system is wrong and some who even advocate the adoption of the British system.

In general, the remedy seems to lie with the Congress —a broader outlook, more information, the abolition of outworn rules and dubious ways—above all, the performance of its proper function: the supervision of the acts of the executive.

Professor Banner of Princeton makes the case strongly: "The scandal of the Presidency has led us to overlook the shoddy practices and effective regulations which have, for too long, characterized the Congress. Both the House and the Senate have made some progress during the past three years in reducing the pall of secrecy and the seniority system that continue to govern it, but scarcely enough to justify the hopes of those who see our salvation in Congressional government. We may not wish for the President we have, but until Congress mends its own ways, who wants the Congress?"

Finally, there should be a good relationship between the President and the press; otherwise, the country will suffer. There is, of course, a natural-adversary attitude between the two; the job of the press is to find out, and at times the administration's job is to conceal; yet, if there are candor and integrity on both sides, they will act as friendly opponents.

There was general agreement that "public support is necessary for effective pursuit of foreign policy objectives," as Zbigniew Brzezinski puts it. This was the view of President Truman, who summed up succinctly and convincingly the problems and the opportunities of the White House in a conversation with Cyrus Sulzberger: "Presidents from the time of George Washington have been subjected to attacks and abuse. It is the way that a free and open society keeps its government institutions on the alert. It is a small price to pay for an aroused and active public opinion. . . . The Presidency, in large measure, depends on the occupant, his scope, his capacity to resist pressures from within and without and, most importantly, a sense of the times, as well as a sense of the future. Above all, the President must communicate with the people, to avoid the risk of a loss of public confidence."

Public Opinion

The improvement of public opinion is a job for the government, for the media, for all the forces of education.

The government must give out more information and more understandable information. The classification system was to have been changed after the Pentagon Papers revelation, but so far there is no evidence that there has been anything approaching the revolution that is needed. Watergate revealed the evils of intrigue and secrecy; that problem, too, is unresolved.

The media must play their part, a large part; they must pay much more attention to international news, print more of it, and make it more understandable. They must convince their readers that there is no such thing as foreign news anymore; it is all local in its way; what is happening in any part of the world affects almost all the other segments.

Basically, the task is to achieve a more informed nation —a process that involves three separate efforts: information must be provided for the people; the people must be engaged, that is, they must use the information; and, most important, the nation's leaders must provide vision and inspiration.

The task of engaging and inspiring the people depends in large part on the President. His assignment is to be President of all the people, to strive for unity, to provide leadership, to inform the nation—in general, to overcome cynicism and distrust. He must appeal to the idealism of the American people and address himself to their human concerns.

As steps toward closing the credibility gap and inspiring trust, the President must take the public more often into his confidence and do much more by way of education and explanation in talks to the nation. He might well arrange more press conferences, speak with more candor to the press, and insist that classification be restricted.

The educational system needs a complete overhauling—of trustee boards, of faculty, of courses, of objectives. The schoolmen must devote themselves to developing rounded men and women and better citizens, rather than specialists.

The task is also one for the Three Estates (the reference is to the three parliamentary components in Britain: Lords, Commons, and Bishops; here it is the Congress) and for the Fourth Estate (the press). In addition, as Betty Friedan suggested, a Fifth Estate should be involved—a new institution to provide participation by the people in governmental decisions and to supply information that will bring about real, not pseudo, national debate.

The Urgent Task

Mr. Hyman finds an eloquent lesson in history: "When on the eve of battle the Spartans made sacrifice to the gods, the honor of the first sacrifice did not go to the god of war, but to the god of poetry, on the theory that however the battle went, the poets would have the last word and they could make a victory into a defeat, a defeat into a victory.

"I wonder whether we cannot reinstate in our own society this tremendously powerful figure of the poet so that no matter what happens in the real world the poet can give us the vision that will correspond with the ideal."

Mr. Hyman added: "There was a law of Rome which I think should be made part of the fundamental law of this country: that it is a crime to despair of the Republic."

Mark Twain supplies a motto for President, for people, for press, for all of us—one that Mr. Truman kept on his desk: "Always do right. This will gratify some people and astonish the rest."

COMMENTARY
by Audrey March

Is an informed public opinion vital to a sound foreign policy? The argument in these pages is that it is. But there are those who contend otherwise. So the debate goes: Would more information, better means of transmission, and more intelligent public debate produce a more successful foreign policy? Or would public participation obfuscate issues and hamper policy-makers?

The answer lies in the key word *informed*. There are two dangers in the public opinion area: first, that the public, lethargic and visionless, will take no interest in foreign affairs, looking upon them as remote or irrelevant; second, that it will move by emotion rather than by logic or reason. In both instances, the only remedy is information.

The course of events is bound to bring a change as international issues impinge more and more on domestic concerns. The rising costs of energy and other raw materials, trade barriers, defense expenditures, the international monetary situation, the decline of American economic influence in many areas will affect the jobs, security, available income, and manner of living of most Americans. Consequently, public opinion is certain to be aroused and pressure on lawmakers will be forthcoming.

Such pressure could force the policy-makers into politically motivated, hastily conceived actions. For example, if the American public, as a result of disillusionment with the recent failures of our diplomacy in Southeast Asia and the Middle East and concern with domestic needs, then demands protectionist, isolationist measures, a withdrawal from international commitments may occur at a time when worldwide cooperation is most needed.

It has happened before. After World War I, Americans turned away from foreign concerns and rejected participation in the League of Nations. During the 1930s, the American public, preoccupied with domestic issues, demanded the maintenance of strict neutrality; according to a Gallup poll taken in December 1939, the dominant foreign affairs issue was still defined as "keeping out of war." (Even after our entrance into the war, three Gallup polls indicated that only small percentages of the American public considered foreign policy problems as the most vital issues. The majority listed inflation, the threat of depression, food shortages, and labor problems as the most important issues facing the nation.)

The history of the 1900s reveals many instances of disastrous failures of public opinion—or lack of public opinion. Had there been an alert and moving opinion, the Vietnam withdrawal might have taken place months, even years, before; the myth of Communism as a monolithic menace would have been punctured long before it was; Fascism in the '30s would have been recognized for the menace that it was; the Tonkin Gulf Resolution, giving the President absolute power, might have been debated and rejected.

What Might Have Been

It is interesting to speculate about what would have happened if, at the time of the escalation of our involvement in Vietnam, the Congress, the media, and the public had all been well informed about the relative importance of Southeast Asia to American security, about our capability of sustaining large-scale, long-term involvement there, and about what would be required in terms of lives, capital, and time, to assure the victory for the government of South Vietnam. Informed public opinion, then, would have made a considerable difference in the policies America pursued during the last decades.

The grave question facing us is how we are to achieve that informed public attitude. If the public will react, the Congress, which controls government appropriations and provides the legal framework for our international commitments, will surely respond.

Such public participation in the foreign policy-making process requires education, information, and leadership. The educational institutions must provide the basic framework with studies of America's role in world affairs. The President and his advisers must mend the enormous credibility gap that has been created in recent years.

Congress, too, must play a vital role in the process. It is not enough for legislators to respond to the attitudes of their constituents or to support or condemn the administration's actions on a partisan basis. They must educate themselves about foreign affairs, develop reasoned, intelligent responses to executive proposals, and inform the public of the reasons for their positions.

The media devote scant attention to foreign affairs, and when they do, often concern themselves as much with trivia as with significant events. What is needed obviously is editorial policy as responsible to the public's need for information as it is responsive to the public's demand for entertainment.

The largest task falls on the American public. No improvement of Presidential leadership, Congressional concern, or media responsibility will amount to anything if the people themselves fail to seek out the information, analyze it, debate it, and then act upon it. Informed and responsive public opinion can make a difference. It can demand that the executive explain how its actions relate to American interests; it can insist that its representatives in Congress inform themselves well enough to be able to form an intelligent response to the administration's proposals.

Informed public opinion is more crucial now than ever before. Americans will be increasingly limited in the actions they may take in world affairs, because of Soviet strength and influence, because of the growing independence of our allies, and because of the demands of Third World countries for higher prices for their raw materials and wider markets for their finished products. More cooperation, because of the threat of nuclear war, and more aid, because of the threat of worldwide famine, are required at a time when many Americans feel we have already cooperated too fully and given too freely.

If the American response is not to be one of belligerent protectionism, disillusioned withdrawal, and hysterical recriminations, then Americans must understand that there are no immediate, short-term, or permanent solutions to international problems; that there are inevitable trade-offs involved in international affairs; and that America, although powerful and influential, cannot impose its might on the whole world. Our true security depends upon the understanding of our strengths and our limits and of the difficult tasks and enormous possibilities that lie before us.

APPENDIX

This is an unusual type of appendix; properly it is not an appendix at all, but a series of original statements that have contributed importantly to the analyses and arguments in the report. It contains the texts of four questionnaires, one addressed to well-known public figures, a second to members of the Congress, a third to authors of books on opinion, and the fourth to the managing editors of the country's largest papers. There is a summary of each questionnaire, followed by the questions and the answers.

QUESTIONNAIRE 1

To National Observers

This questionnaire was answered by the following:

180

Ben Bagdikian, author and media critic
Thomas Bailey, author and historian
Ben Bradlee, Executive Editor, *Washington Post*
Zbigniew Brzezinski, Director, Research Institute on International Change, Columbia University
James McGregor Burns, Professor of Political Science, Williams College
Joan Gans Cooney, President, Children's Television Workshop
Phillips Davison, Professor, School of Journalism, Columbia University
Charles Frankel, Professor of Philosophy and Public Affairs, Columbia University
Wes Gallagher, President and General Manager of Associated Press
George Gallup, Director, American Institute of Public Opinion
Doris Graber, Professor of Political Science, University of Illinois
Henry Graff, Professor of History, Columbia University
W. Averell Harriman, former Ambassador, government official
Roger Hilsman, author and educator
Anthony Lewis, columnist, *New York Times*
Marya Mannes, author
Ithiel deSola Pool, Professor of Communications, Massachusetts Institute of Technology
George Reedy, Dean, College of Journalism, Marquette University
Edwin Reischauer, former Ambassador to Japan
Dean Rusk, Professor of Law, University of Georgia
C. L. Sulzberger, columnist, *New York Times*
David Truman, President, Mount Holyoke College

Daniel Yankelovich, President, Yankelovich, Skelly & White

Summary

This questionnaire brought some fascinating suggestions and demonstrated how difficult it is to pin down an exact definition of public opinion. The difficulty is due to the dearth of monolithic opinion; instead, there is usually a combination of separate viewpoints.

However, there are good attempts at definition. For example, George Reedy puts it this way: "Public opinion is a consensus of individual attitudes of sufficient size to initiate, influence, sustain, diminish or block social action." Or George Gallup, who goes back to James Bryce, calls it "the aggregate of the views men hold regarding matters that affect or interest the community."

A second point of agreement is that there cannot be opinion—this is Yankelovich's view—unless people have a grasp of the issue, unless they feel strongly about it, and unless their viewpoint is the product of thought and not emotion.

Yankelovich makes another fascinating point, that the most useful service of opinion surveys is to provide an assessment of how the public is likely to react to events that have not yet taken place. This could be, of course, of cardinal importance to the decision-maker.

Doris Graber adds this caveat: that political leaders frequently make assertions about public opinion when there is little evidence to support their statements, even though they gain currency because of propaganda and the prestige of the spokesman.

There are, however, those who have fundamental doubts about the polls. For example, Tony Lewis says: "Public opinion is the body of belief in the community on any issue. In foreign affairs, however, it may often be only the informed opinion that one considers since so many are neither informed or interested." And Ben Bradlee says, "Public opinion should be mistrusted since there are so many publics and they have such ill-defined opinions."

The group was challenged to cite instances when opinion failed to function. Vietnam, of course, was mentioned most often as the outstanding example in which public opinion might have forced a reversal of policy and failed to do so. There are other historic examples. "In the 1930s when the nation was facing a resurgent Germany and Japan public opinion was becoming increasingly isolationist" (Burns). "Lack of desire to feed the starving in other countries"" (Mannes). "It would have been useful if the public had comprehended the menace of Fascism at an earlier date" (Reedy). Other instances cited were failure to mobilize opinion against "Hitler's persecution of the Jews and Indochina's slaughter of the Chinese" (Graff).

An interesting difference of opinion developed over the value of public opinion. Mrs. Cooney said she wasn't sure that public opinion was "useful" when it came to foreign affairs. Mr. Bradlee held that "public opinion is floundering in a sea of emotion rather than knowledge" and is therefore ineffective. On the other hand, George Gallup believes that public opinion fails far less than the leadership in foreign affairs. "The public is sometimes ready for policy changes before the administration and the new China policy, for example, should have been started long before Nixon began it."

The third question raised the issue of the public's knowledge of current affairs. This led to a sharp division of opinion. Mr. Rusk takes a middle ground: "I am convinced that the American people are better informed about world affairs than are the people of any other country I know, but we still need to do much more because of the inevitable role and influence of the United States in the world about us."

Mr. Brzezinski casts a negative vote: "Public opinion is not well informed about foreign affairs because they are too complex and require a subtle understanding of the nuances." Mr. Gallagher: "The public is better informed about public affairs than at any time in our history. At the present time the economic conditions take priority." Mr. Bradlee: "Public opinion is rarely well informed about anything. The issues of our day are all so complicated that there is little true understanding, various biases are served by special publications and real knowledge is hard to obtain."

The panel was then asked how much a policy-maker should be influenced by what he judges public opinion to be. This is really two questions: first, how does he judge what public opinion is; second, how much attention does he pay to it?

As for the first, he uses the polls, he talks to people, he gets letters, and eventually he plays a hunch unless, as in the case of Vietnam, the evidence is overwhelming. As to the influence of public opinion on foreign policy, the President obviously must pay attention to it if only to ascertain the strength of the opposition.

Again the question of education comes up. If the President advocates some measure or some action and there is obviously public resistance to it, the President has to do a job of education, and if he does not succeed he has to pull back, as Roosevelt did in 1937 when he asserted our rights on the high seas against the U-boats.

Finally the question was put: "What can be done to educate the public in foreign affairs?" Mr. Hilsman: "It requires only that members of Congress, the press and others most directly involved have the courage to exercise the power they already have. This, in turn, requires that they have the vigorous support, not of the entire public, but at least a small, intelligent, well informed, attentive public." Dr. Gallup calls for the education of the public, beginning with the elementary grades—a section on geography and history with periods spent abroad. Mr. Harriman: "The Congress and the American people should be brought more effectively into this discussion. I urge that there be full disclosure and declassification of all the information relative to our nuclear capability and all the facts we have about those of the Soviet Union."

Mr. Brzezinski: "The assignment of educating the public ought to be undertaken much more deliberately and on a much more continuous basis by the President himself and this could encourage others to address themselves more to the central issues." Mr. Gallagher says it is up to the press "to translate foreign affairs into meaningful terms of human relationships and common problems." Mr. Rusk advocates more discussion of foreign affairs in the institutions of learning and in the general organizations outside the schools.

Mr. Davison is doubtful that the whole community should be involved in foreign affairs; however, according to Miss Mannes, courses in foreign affairs should be mandatory in the whole educational system. Mr. Bagdikian urges that we: "Educate political leaders on the long-range needs of the whole American public rather than only the most powerful corporate and bureaucratic desires."

The Text

This is the full text of the questions and answers:

(1) *How would you define public opinion?*

Bagdikian: That collection of attitudes and beliefs held by members of the public—in varying degrees of intensity and with varying configurations at different times—which at any point of decision may crystallize to a degree at which it can be tested or express itself in some outward behavior.

Bailey: Public opinion is the opinion at a given time of the public at large, excluding those who have no opinion on a given subject, and including press opinion, pressure-group opinion, et cetera. Press opinion must not be confused with public opinion. Public opinion is often held privately and frequently finds no public expression.

Bradlee: I would define public opinion as what a definable segment of the American people thinks it knows at any given time. Public opinion should be mistrusted, since there are so many publics and they have such ill-defined opinions.

Brzezinski: As broadly shared on highly generalized views on issues of common concern, usually without too much expert knowledge.

Burns: As clusters of attitudes on the part of the mass public, as mobilized by leaders and structured by political, economic, and social institutions.

Cooney: I think public opinion is just what the words imply. It is the shared opinions, feelings, and attitudes held by a sizable or, at least, measurable segment of the public. How these attitudes, opinions, and feelings are formed remains something of a mystery. Certainly the editorial pages of newspapers do not necessarily reflect public opinion or even shape it. Information delivered by the print and electronic media certainly affects opinions but not always in predictable ways. For example, until recently at least, presidential views tended to have more effect on public opinion than the media, particularly in regard to foreign policy.

Davison: It is a consensus, involving substantial numbers of individual opinions, on a public issue. This consensus is formed as a result of intercommunication and has the power to exert social pressure, to a greater or lesser extent, on those who are a part of it and those who are outside it. Thus there can be several public opinions on a given public issue, although one can sometimes speak of a dominant public opinion.

Frankel: There is an "inner harbor" of "public opinion" —the opinions of knowledgeable, informed, and influential people, who are not themselves directly involved in making the decisions, with respect to a given subject. There is an "outer harbor"—the opinions of influential people who have "clout" over a wide range of issues—exempli gratia, well-known columnists and commentators, editors, political figures, industrial and labor leaders, et al. Finally, there is more general opinion, which shows up in votes, polls, collective moods, et cetera. Even here, it is worthwhile distinguishing between people who are affected by a policy—exempli gratia, people with families abroad who are concerned about immigration laws—and people who are simply responding to what they read or see on television. This last category, composed of the affected and the relatively unaffected but sporadically interested, may be called the "ocean" of public opinion. It may not make much difference day by day, but over the long run the movement of the tides in the "ocean" does have its effects; there are moments of sudden eruption when the "ocean" takes over like a tidal wave.

Gallagher: Public opinion is divided on any number of subjects all the time. I would define public opinion as that view with which the majority of the public agree on any given subject.

Gallup: Many persons have tried to define public opinion. The simplest definition is "the sum total of individual views." Or as James Bryce said, "the aggregate of the views men hold regarding matters that affect or interest the community."

Graff: Public opinion is the least common denominator of the people's attitude on this or that.

Lewis: The body of belief in the community on any issue. In foreign affairs, it may often be only informed opinion that one considers, since many are neither informed nor interested.

Mannes: A doubtful consensus of a splintered plurality as derived by polls of "average" Americans in all walks of life—actually the expression of a syncopated chorus who think that they know what they think. Very few do, or are in a position to express it.

Pool: Opinion may mean attitudes on policy, reactions to events; public may mean expressed in public about *res publica*. Take your choice.

Reedy: Public opinion is a consensus of individual attitudes of sufficient size to initiate, influence, sustain, diminish, or block social action. It is never monolithic but is best considered in terms of vectoring as practiced by physicists—a collection of forces veering in the same direction and mutually influencing each other. Furthermore, *effective* public opinion is not solely a question of numbers, for the factor of intensity must be taken into account. There are occasions in which a sizable minority will dominate the majority because the majority simply does not care enough about the issue or does not have sufficient status in society to make its will felt.

Reischauer: As expressed in publications and TV by an interested, articulate minority; as mirrored in the vote by the total voting public.

Truman: On the matter of a definition of public opinion, I find no reason materially to modify the definition that I arrived at when I published my book *The Governmental Process* in 1951. That definition is approximately as follows: "The opinions of the aggregate of individuals making up the public under discussion concerning the issue or situation that defines them as a public." I have further defined the public, following John Dewey, as "an aggregate of individuals who are aware, or who can be made aware, of an issue or action, real or contemplated."

Yankelovich: It is almost impossible to compress a definition of public opinion into a few brief paragraphs, but here goes:

To avoid being too abstract, let me try to build up a definition from a few examples. Let us consider public opinion on subjects such as abortion, capital punishment, and Mr. Ford's conduct of the presidency.

1. Public opinion on these matters always involves a *cognitive* aspect, id est, people must know what abortion means, what capital punishment means, and hold at least some vague conception of what Mr. Ford has been doing.

2. In each instance there is also an *affective* aspect, id est, strong feelings are generated by subjects such as abortion and capital punishment.

3. There is always a *judgmental* aspect, id est, people are obligated to make a decision or judgment for or against the issue, irrespective of the conflicts, ambivalences, and contradictions that may underlie their judgments. If the public's attitudes, values, and emotions on a subject are so vague and diffuse that they have not been crystallized into judgmental form, it is probably not meaningful to speak of public opinion on that subject.

4. Public opinion always refers to *shared* meanings and excludes private personal meanings. Thus, a person may be bitterly opposed to capital punishment because a rela-

tive who was later proved innocent had been executed. This background of personal meanings is excluded from public opinion. His judgment is given equal weight to that of the person who may be opposed for purely impersonal reasons. Thus, one key aspect of public opinion is to isolate the attitudes, values, beliefs, and judgments that are shared in common with others from those that are private and personal.

5. The most critical and subtle point to be made about public opinion concerns an assessment of how the public is likely to react to events that have not yet taken place. For example, what would public opinion be if Mr. Ford intervened militarily in the event of a new Arab oil embargo? Thus, public opinion covers *potential* public response as well as actual public response to an issue. This, in my view, is a point of cardinal importance, with far-reaching implications for how public opinion is gauged.

In the light of the above, I would define public opinion as (a) a body of shared attitudes, values, beliefs, and feelings, (b) focused on a specific issue, (c) sufficiently crystallized so that people's judgments can be gauged, (d) where the viewpoint of the public is understood in sufficient depth to enable one to make a forecast about the public's likely behavior if confronted with events that have not yet taken place.

To avoid misunderstanding, two additional points must be made. Most public opinion polls do not, in the light of this definition, measure public opinion in the full sense of the term. They measure surface aspects of it, but usually not in sufficient depth to illuminate its true nature. Also, the conventional use of the term *opinion* is misleading. In conventional usage, opinion is contrasted with, and distinguished from, attitudes, values, and feelings. I am using the term to include, rather than to exclude, these aspects of shared consciousness.

(2) *Can you cite instances in which public opinion about foreign affairs failed to function at a time when it could have been useful?*

Bagdikian: The Vietnam war almost from the beginning, because of misinformation or lack of information received from political leaders and the news media.

Bailey: The best example I can cite of a nonfunctioning opinion relates to Nixon's policy of a four-year withdrawal of American troops from Vietnam. He clearly had the acquiescent support of a majority of the American public. He applauded the patience of the great "silent majority," which outnumbered the vocal and angry minority of doves. Too many of the great silent majority had swallowed the line that Communism was a monolithic menace, and that if we failed in Vietnam we would all soon be fighting on the beaches of Waikiki.

Bradlee: Certainly American public opinion about Vietnam failed to function for a long time when it could have been useful, although it finally functioned usefully. I suspect public opinion about the Middle East right now is foundering in a sea of emotion rather than knowledge.

Brzezinski: Yes, at the time of the American engagement in Vietnam, or more likely with regard to the misconception of the anachronistic character of the Nixon-Kissinger foreign policy.

Burns: In the 1930s, when the nation was facing a resurgent Germany and Japan and public opinion was becoming increasingly isolationist.

Cooney: I'm not sure that public opinion is "useful" when it comes to the conduct of foreign affairs. However, had public opinion been mobilized effectively, I believe the Vietnam War would have ended three or four years earlier than it did. I certainly believe it would have been useful had public opinion made it impossible for President Johnson to commit large numbers of American troops to Southeast Asia. However, one wonders if a well-informed public opinion would be "useful" in the Middle East and in what way. Could a well-informed public have stopped the Russian wheat deal, which has created so much inflation in the U.S.? I don't know.

Davison: Well-developed public opinion sometimes fails to form on a crucial issue. This was probably the case prior to the Bay of Pigs invasion of Cuba; it probably has been true with respect to Middle East policy prior to the October War.

Frankel: In 1965, public opinion ("inner harbor") and public opinion ("ocean") was not so convinced about the wisdom or morality of Vietnam policy as most of the "outer harbor." Doubts, however, were not effectively marshaled or expressed. Again, in relation to the Nixon Administration's economic moves against Japan, public opinion has been unhappily quiescent even though we risk pushing Japan (and eventually ourselves) into disruptive forms of economic protectionism. Ditto policies toward Western Europe.

Gallagher: Public opinion divided on the Vietnam war.

If at that time there had been a real consensus and pressure on public officials, the United States might not have entered that war.

Gallup: Public opinion fails far less often than leadership in dealing with foreign affairs. The U.S. would have ended both the Vietnam and Korean Wars two years earlier if public opinion had been followed by the nation's leadership. When public opinion fails, it is usually because of an almost total lack of information on the part of the public. Examples: Bay of Pigs, Tonkin Gulf.

Graff: At the beginning of Hitler's persecution of the Jews; at the time of Indochina's slaughter of the Chinese.

Lewis: The outstanding example is of course Vietnam. Tragedy for both Indochina and the United States might have been avoided if American opinion had understood earlier that the U.S. was waging an aggressive war on its own initiative and against its true interest. The public is not to be blamed for its tardiness, because successive Presidents concealed the facts and nature of the war.

Mannes: Those Americans capable of forming a position on foreign affairs are few or quiet. Other lands are far away; we are physically contained and often apathetic to distant problems, however severe. We look at the starving far away, and eat as we always have. The apathy to amnesty is one strange, massive condition and the lack of desire to feed the starving in many countries is another one.

Reedy: This is a difficult question because it involves a value judgment as to what is "useful." From my standpoint, it would have been useful had the public comprehended the menace of Fascism at an earlier date. From my standpoint, it would be very useful if the public had a better comprehension of Latin America.

Yankelovich: Lyndon Johnson was misled by the polls into believing that the public supported his Vietnam policy at a time when it had, in fact, developed serious doubts and reservations about it. Another example: The public was ready for a new China policy long before Nixon started one. Another instance: Up to the recent fuss about inflation, which has turned the country inward, the public was ready for bolder risks for peace than the administration has been willing to take.

(3) *How well informed is public opinion about foreign affairs? If you feel it is ignorant or apathetic, to what do you ascribe this?*

Bagdikian: I find this impossible to answer because "foreign affairs" covers such a vast collection of issues and these issues vary so widely in their relevancy, real and perceived, that no generalization can be drawn on the whole field as seen by the whole population. The general public depends on its most visible public leaders and its news media to set the agenda of importance and priorities in foreign affairs and in general it is the political leaders and the news media who are deficient or self-serving in this matter.

Bailey: Generally the public is ill-informed about foreign affairs, and even those leaders in Washington who are supposed to know make the wrong choices on the basis of the mass of evidence available to them. Too much of the public is ill-informed because of ignorance, illiteracy, apathy, and preoccupation with daily pursuits and pleasures. The failure to acquire proper information may be due to such factors as poor education, a feeling that expressing one's opinion in public will not do any good, and a conviction that the "smart" men whom we elect to high office know best because they have all the information that is necessary.

Bradlee: Public opinion is rarely well informed about anything, I'm afraid I have come to believe. The issues of our day, and their solutions—the economy, energy, détente, business, journalism—are all so complicated that there is little true understanding. Various biases are served by special publications, and true knowledge is hard to obtain.

I would suspect that public opinion is better informed about foreign affairs than it has been, largely due to the impact of Vietnam, and President Nixon's successes in China. But if you mean by "well informed" a degree of knowledge that you have, I suspect that the public is ill informed.

Brzezinski: Public opinion is not well informed about foreign affairs because they are too complex and require a subtle understanding of the nuances. In other words, there is an inherent problem here.

Burns: Public opinion is well informed about foreign affairs when leaders sharpen the issues clearly and responsibly. It is ignorant or apathetic to the degree that leaders obscure the issues and resort to such doctrines as "bipartisan foreign policy" in an effort to escape legitimate conflict and debate.

Cooney: Public opinion, among the better educated, is

probably reasonably well informed about foreign affairs. However, I believe that it is apathetic and that the reasons are directly traceable to the Vietnam war, compounded by the Middle East crises. In the first case, informed public opinion failed to bring the war to a halt and, in the second, a consensus among the informed has been too difficult to come by. In other words, for various reasons, I think that most people who care about foreign affairs feel absolutely helpless about affecting foreign policy in any way.

Davison: Bodies of public opinion on foreign affairs range from those who are well informed to those who are very poorly informed; some are vigorous, some apathetic. There are many reasons for ignorance or apathy among those who should be concerned with an issue. They may be poorly informed about the issue; the relevance of the issue to them may not be clear; or there may be no channels, or insufficient channels, through which they can exchange ideas.

Frankel: With regard to the larger orientations of foreign policy, public opinion ("outer harbor" and "ocean") is informed, but it tends to fall into rigid molds, thereby reinforcing the rigidities of the policy-makers and experts. Sloganeering, including the sloganeering and excessive simplifications of the press, has much to do with this. Another factor is that vested interest—emotional, economic, professional—plays a much larger role in "inner" and "outer harbor" opinion than is commonly recognized, and tends to spread outward into the "ocean."

Gallagher: I don't think the public is ignorant of public affairs, quite the contrary. They are probably better informed than at any time in our history. I do not think, however, that they are giving a high priority to foreign affairs at the present time because of the economic conditions in this country, which affect them directly and take priority. They would, for example, have a high interest in what the Arab oil states are doing because it affects economic conditions here, but they would be little interested in whether Italy has a new government.

Gallup: The public is not so well informed about foreign affairs as it should be. My opinion is that not enough emphasis is given in the public schools or in college to such subjects as geography, history, and political science.

Graff: Most Americans until recently have responded to foreign affairs as a function of their ancestral connections to the "old country." As long as the national interests remain fuzzy, opinion will be apathetic.

Lewis: Generally not well informed, perhaps because foreign affairs understandably seem remote and complicated. But when public interests are strongly engaged, as in Vietnam or an oil embargo, public concern and attention naturally increase.

Mannes: It is still possible for a majority of Americans to skip the foreign news in their papers and magazines, and merely get snippets on television or radio and feel informed. What results is not ignorance—they have all the major information and arguments on papers or on TV and radio—if they look or listen to news in the first place. Perhaps there are too many spigots washing their brains by continuous entertainment and escape. It has been my opinion for many years that the worst thing to happen was the union of news with commercial sponsors, thus making news a part of the entertainment.

Pool: The old cliché "no Congressman was ever beaten on foreign policy" is easily rebutted by reference to Vietnam or the tariff. The usual answer is "but that is domestic." So if we define domestic policy as anything that touches the voter directly, and foreign as that which doesn't affect him, is there any wonder that the voter is uninvolved in foreign policy?

Reedy: In my judgment public opinion is reasonably coherent where Europe is concerned; becoming somewhat coherent where Eastern Asia is concerned; inflamed in terms of the Middle East; largely uninterested in South America (except for some negative attitudes) ; and almost totally ignorant concerning Africa. I attribute this situation to the statistical fact that most of us have European forebears; to the direct impact that has been made upon our daily lives in the past few years by Eastern Asia and the Middle East; to the lack of contact with the Latin nations other than Mexico; and to the romanticization of Africa by the blacks.

Reischauer: On most issues it is apathetic because of ignorance both as to the facts and the relevance of the issues to the U.S. and their personal lives. The basic problem is education in the broadest sense.

Rusk: There are inherent limitations upon the ability of the ordinary citizen to know about foreign affairs. Newspapers have limited space, the electronic media have even more limited time, and the citizen himself must get on with the day's work. Nevertheless, the citizen can and does play a crucial role in determining the main directions of policy, even if he cannot follow the thousand cables a day that go out of the Department of State on every working day. The problem is not secrecy—secrets are a tiny fraction of the business of foreign policy. The problem is the mass of relevant information that is available and needed for considered judgment on matters of detail.

In general, I am convinced that the American people are better informed about world affairs than are the people of any other country I know, but we still need to do much more because of the inevitable role and influence of the United States in the world about us. What used to be a good idea is now a harsh necessity because we cannot solve our urgent national problems without a large degree of international action—whether we are talking about inflation, energy, raw materials, the environment, the population explosion, the international monetary system, or any other of our so-called domestic problems.

Yankelovich: Not very well informed. At the moment the public is preoccupied with domestic affairs. But even when it is not, its lack of information comes from two sources: the failure to see the relevance of foreign-policy issues to the average person's daily life, and the public's feelings of inadequacy about making judgments on foreign affairs, leaving this domain to the "experts".

(4) *How much should a policy-maker, from the President down, be influenced by what he judges public opinion to be?*

Bagdikian: Ultimately he needs to judge what is the long-range benefit of foreign policy on the welfare of the public. So first he needs to know the long-range needs of the public, which is a subject that he may not be able to decide in the abstract. He also needs to know how much the public understands about a particular policy, since he may fail by neglecting to provide full information and a fair presentation of alternatives. There are times when he must act without doing these things and in that case he is obligated to present a full and fair retrospective picture as soon as possible.

Bailey: As long as we have a democracy the policy-makers must give much heed to what the people want and particularly what they stand for. If a given policy is clearly in the national interest, the policy-makers should make the necessary effort to "sell" it to the mass of the people. Roosevelt tried to alert the people to the Nazi menace and to the imminent collapse of democracy abroad, but failed to budge the mass of isolationists. He therefore contrived to "do good by stealth" and cause the Germans to appear to be the aggressors. (Johnson did the same thing in connection with the Tonkin Gulf affair.) A case can be made out for the father-knows-best approach, but more convincingly if that policy turns out for the best.

Bradlee: A policy-maker must be influenced by public opinion only when public opinion looks as if it would prevent a policy-maker from doing what should be done. I suspect that the trouble comes—certainly it has come in recent years—when a policy-maker tries to convince the public it has an opinion that in fact it does not hold.

Brzezinski: To the extent that public support is necessary for effective pursuit of foreign-policy objectives.

Burns: He should be significantly influenced by public opinion to the extent he feels that it is informed. He can ignore existing public opinion to a considerable degree, but he must be prepared to meet the demands of public opinion once he has acted. In short, he should have a good deal of leeway in developing policy, but must be prepared to suffer the consequences of that public opinion, especially at election time.

Cooney: Policy-makers, particularly elected policy-makers, cannot help but be influenced by public opinion. Probably there are times when great leaders go against public opinion, or rather, can't develop public opinion fast enough for the moves that must be made. But I think it is probably a mistake for an elected U.S. official, namely the President, to try to conduct foreign policy without keeping public opinion with him. Since the presidency, in my view, has more effect on shaping public opinion of foreign policy and foreign policy itself than any other institution or group of institutions in this country, there seems very little excuse not to lead public opinion in the areas of foreign policy.

Thus the President, in particular, very seldom needs to make any foreign-policy move without a consensus supporting him. A President who cannot keep public opinion with him in foreign policy (President Johnson comes to mind immediately; President Truman is another example) will probably decide not to run again or will be defeated. It's interesting to note that "small" wars out in Southeast Asia (too complicated for American public opinion) brought both men to low points in public opinion polls, affecting their decisions to run or not to run.

Davison: The policy-maker should certainly take public opinion into account as one factor to be weighed, along with others. The weight to be assigned to it would vary with its size and quality, but especially the latter.

Frankel: Obviously, he has to take its political significance into account. The Vietnam War, which the Johnson Administration tried to fight without rationing, significant tax increases, or a genuinely universal conscription policy, was an effort to avoid the political costs by, as it were, sneaking the war past public opinion before it took notice. The policy could work only if the war could be won in a hurry. Since the Pentagon Papers show that the decision-makers were aware that the war would probably be long and difficult, this choice of tactics must be called politically irresponsible. Public opinion should have been taken into account—and if the policy-makers decided that the war was really vital enough to our interests to risk initial public doubt and subsequent public disapproval, they should have made the effort, through genuine debate, to marshal an informed opinion on their side.

This raises the question of whether policy-makers should turn to public opinion not simply in a political perspective, but to receive guidance and instruction. The answer to the question is complicated. Sometimes expert opinion is better informed, braver, less stereotyped, than reigning opinion in a government. But sometimes the reverse is true. Again, "oceanic" opinion may simply be the watered version of experts' and influentials' regnant views. Sometimes, however, there is a vein of common sense to it, of opinion uncluttered by vanity and immediate vested interest and far enough away from the problem to see its main lines rather than its confusing and comparatively insignificant details. A policy-maker ought to have his eye peeled for these cracks and divisions in public opinion, and he ought never to assume that any one of the groups ("inner," "outer," "oceanic") has a monopoly of wisdom. If he leans, as LBJ did, on a narrow band of putative expert opinion, he is in for a rude awakening.

Gallagher: The President or policy-maker must be influenced by what he considers public opinion to be because if he goes against public opinion on a major issue his policy will fail. There may be narrow issues in which the President would not be influenced by public opinion on the side of justice, but if it is the type of subject that needs public support it would be futile for him to try to carry out a policy the public does not believe in, such as prohibition, an unpopular war, etcetera.

Gallup: A President shouldn't be "influenced" by what he judges public opinion to be, but he should be guided by it. If he thinks the public is wrong, then it is his duty to inform or instruct the public as to why it is wrong. Certainly, in a democracy, he should pay attention to the views of the people.

Graff: The President and all policy-makers must create the public opinion that is required. It never exists independently.

Hilsman: It has often been said that no citizen can possibly keep himself equally well informed on all subjects of public policy; they are obviously too many and too complex. But this does not mean that well-informed, attentive publics are not vital to enlightened policy and especially to foreign affairs. Presidents, like princes, tend to isolate themselves, to limit the people giving them advice to those who offer what they want to hear, and Presidents have more power to do this in foreign affairs than in domestic. In reflecting on our policy in Southeast Asia over the past few years, for example, I thought Kennedy's policy of neutralizing Laos in 1962 was wise and Johnson's policy of escalating the struggle in Vietnam in 1965 was unwise, but I was very uneasy indeed that both men were completely free to follow their own whims rather than have their judgments subjected to debate and approval by other parts of government and the public.

Lewis: It is impossible to generalize. He must take opinion into account but also lead. Perhaps the answer is that he must share his knowledge with the Congress, so there can be informed opinion.

Mannes: The policy-makers should be free to have many more contacts with the thinkers and creators in our midst. They should be able to spend at least one week closeted with the best minds and talents in the country and learning the options and the way to use them—a sort of political and humanistic MacDowell Colony intercourse. The President should know how the many different voices can become a functioning chorus—which he hears as well as being a contributor, pro or con. A President should be influenced not by the polls but by individuals in many disciplines who express clear choices for his judgments and actions. Ignorance and apathy of the public are directly related to the acts and words of their leaders. They are also related to the gross undereducation in their schools.

Pool: Let him worry about what public opinion will be! There is no reward to being in agreement with public opinion if later the public changes its mind.

Reedy: A policy-maker cannot permit public opinion to be the sole determinant of policy, and frequently the policy-maker is compelled to act before public opinion has been formed. But every policy-maker should be aware of the fact no policy can be successful if public opinion digs in its heels and resists.

Reischauer: He must be closely aware of what public opinion, especially as expressed through the Congress, will support, and if support is lacking for essential policies, he should attempt to educate the public.

Yankelovich: In a democracy, he must take public opinion into account. On matters that concern the future well-being of this and other nations, the policy-maker must give the public an opportunity to express its basic goals and values in the form of trade-offs and risks the public is willing or not willing to accept. The public will often leave the means of accomplishing agreed-upon objectives to "experts" and elected representatives, but on basic values the viewpoint of the public should be considered as all-important; otherwise the policy-maker is exceeding his mandate.

(5) *What can be done to educate the public in foreign affairs?*

Bagdikian: Educate political leaders on the long-range needs of the whole American public rather than merely the most powerful corporate and bureaucratic desires. And create a much larger pool of scholars and news people who are expert in foreign affairs, and report on them regularly without dependence on official sources for priorities, values, and major facts.

Bailey: As for the education of the public, I would suggest more programs on radio and TV, the universal media, involving informed people. Making available the basic facts on a day-to-day basis is not enough. Reading the foreign affairs material in the *New York Times* (and absorbing it) is a demanding daily task that is beyond the reach of most people. The problems of foreign affairs today are so complex, what with some forty U.S. alliances, that even the experts cannot grasp all aspects in detail. John Doe simply throws up his hands in despair. At the educational level, we need more exposure to courses relating to international affairs; at the popular level, more exposure in interesting and intelligible form to programs on radio and television. We need many more programs like The Washington Week in Review. The dial-turner may stumble onto them while looking for "All in the Family," before or after.

Brzezinski: I think this function ought to be undertaken much more deliberately and on a more continuous basis by the President himself, and this would encourage others to address themselves more to the central issues.

Burns: This is not easy to answer in a short compass. My central thesis is still that we should define the issues and debate them—it is well-organized political conflict that educates the public most effectively, I feel.

Cooney: There is simply no substitute for better newspapers and electronic reporting on foreign affairs. While the *New York Times* leaves much to be desired when it comes to reporting foreign affairs, it is shocking to realize that it represents, without a doubt, the best foreign-affairs reporting going on in daily newspapers in the United States. Out of New York, unless one buys *Time* Magazine, for example, and watches a network news show each night, one gets practically no foreign affairs reporting because of the failure of the vast majority of newspapers to pay much attention to anything but domestic and local affairs. In addition, we need vastly more interpretation in both electronic and print media (with connection made for us between our own lives and what happens in foreign affairs). Even though audiences for documentaries on television are small by comparison to, say, "All in the Family," such audiences actually number in the millions. The electronic media and the print media seem to have abdicated virtually all responsibility for interpreting foreign affairs for the American public.

Davison: I'm not convinced that the entire public ever can or should be involved in public opinion on all foreign-affairs issues. One avenue to increasing involvement of educated or potentially affected members of the public would be: (a) improvement of area study centers at universities and elsewhere and (b) closer collaboration between these centers and the serious mass media.

Frankel: As the saying goes, "Practice, practice!" Most of all, the public needs to be brought in touch with "public opinion" in the other sectors. The experts should know the ocean, and vice versa. The press's role should be to bring major opinion to the light of day, including major options as the experts, the influentials, the affected publics, and the onlooking public see them.

Gallagher: I think the public has all the information on foreign affairs it can handle at the present time. I think it is up to the press to translate foreign affairs into meaningful terms of human relationships and common problems that stretch across nations' boundaries, rather than concentrating on individual government reactions.

Gallup: The education of the public should begin in the elementary grades with thorough instruction in geography. This should be followed by history. At the level of higher education, every student should be permitted, maybe required, to spend one semester abroad. The actual cost, including transportation, would be no greater than what the student presently spends for one semester on an American campus. And I'm certain that time spent abroad would be far more instructive. The United States could send one or two million students each year to Europe and to the other areas of the world in the nontourist season, with supervised instruction (not necessarily in foreign universities) at a cost no greater than $750 per student.

Graff: As the world continues to become smaller and more interdependent, the public will respond.

Harriman: The bargaining chip theory should be abandoned. The Congress and the American people should be brought more effectively into the discussion. I therefore urge that there be full disclosure and declassification of all information relative to our nuclear capability and all the facts we have about that of the Soviet Union. Obviously I am not referring to secret information about weapons design. Freer and better-informed discussions in the Congress and by the public would make more difficult what seems to be the current practice of releasing only the information to support the military appropriations requests.

Hilsman: Correcting the situation does not really require fundamental changes in our Constitution and political process. It requires only that members of the Congress, the press, and others most directly involved have the courage to exercise the powers they already have. But this in turn requires that they have the active, vigorous support, not of the entire public but at least of a small, intelligent, well-informed, vigorous, and attentive public.

Lewis: It seems to me that the answer to this, as to (4), really amounts to: Fight secrecy. When decisions are made by the Executive branch in secret, as in Vietnam or Chile or 100 other examples, neither the public nor its representatives in the Congress can participate—and can hardly be blamed for taking no interest. Share knowledge and you share responsibility.

Mannes: One foreign language should be a required course in all public schools. Tours to Europe should end with a complete résumé of the students' reactions, written down. Such courses on foreign affairs should be followed in the colleges as mandatory. In either case, the government should contribute most of the cost.

Reedy: In a formal sense, nothing that is not being done now. This is not the type of education that can be forced upon people. What is happening, however, is that foreign affairs are impinging upon Americans with greater impact and they are seeking answers. This means that they are becoming increasingly receptive to information and I believe that the various organizations which stimulate discussion in this field are going to find increasing audiences.

Reischauer: The President and government leaders can do more than they have (this is what leadership really is), but basically it is a problem that formal education, mass media, and the informed minority in the public must do more about.

Rusk: It would help if the news media could spend more space and time in providing more background information, but the real answer lies in what educators call Lifetime Learning. It is easy to say that our schools and colleges should provide more information on world affairs, but that raises difficult questions about how best to use the student time available to teachers and professors. One possibility would be to encourage habits of reading about world affairs on an avocational basis and in injecting world affairs more frequently into the tens of thousands of meetings held in this country every day by civic clubs, professional organizations, and other private groups that meet regularly throughout the year.

Sulzberger: I can only say that the public should be encouraged to read more and more, listen more and more, and argue more and more on the subject of "foreign affairs" which, in the end, may bring the answer to the question of whether we survive or not as a nation.

Yankelovich: A great deal more than is being done now. How to carry this out is too complicated to set down here.

QUESTIONNAIRE 2

To Foreign Affairs Committees of the Congress
The questionnaire was answered by the following:

Foreign Relations Committee of the Senate:

Clifford P. Case, New Jersey
Frank Church, Idaho
George McGovern, South Dakota
Edmund S. Muskie, Maine
Claiborne Pell, Rhode Island
John Sparkman, Alabama
Stuart Symington, Missouri

Foreign Affairs Committee of the House of Representatives:

Jonathan Bingham, New York
William S. Broomfield, Michigan
J. Herbert Burke, Florida
Edward J. Derwinski, Illinois
Pierre S. DuPont, Delaware
Dante B. Fascell, Florida
Paul Findley, Illinois
L. H. Fountain, North Carolina
Donald Fraser, Minnesota
Benjamin A. Gilman, New York
Michael J. Harrington, Massachusetts
Leo J. Ryan, California
Lester Wolff, New York

Summary
The questionnaire addressed to the Congress indicates
that in the area of foreign policy there is only limited com-

munication between members and their constituents. This is surprising because, of those who were asked whether an informed opinion is vital to a sound foreign policy, only two replied in the negative.

Asked: "How well informed is the American public?," only four answered "well informed"; four said "poorly informed"; and seven said "moderately knowledgeable." Of course, critics might raise questions about the state of Congressional information, and express doubt that most members are sufficiently informed to pass judgment on the public.

Another member felt that the public was better informed than ever before, but he added the significant point that the need for it is more critical than ever. A second Congressman adroitly answered: "as well as the media cover news events."

The third question was: "What can be done to improve opinion?" An overwhelming majority answered, "the media." What in the main was not taken into account was that if the media fail in this respect, one cause is their difficulty in obtaining information from two important sources, the White House and Capitol Hill. Only one member referred to "unnecessary secrecy."

The fourth question dealt with the amount of attention paid to public opinion by the Executive and the Congress. The answer generally was, "a great deal," and many members added "much more by the Congress than the Executive." (One remarked, "Secretary Kissinger is obviously indifferent to public opinion.") Representative Fraser made a significant point in discussing the factors that influence policy. He spoke of the "foreign-policy constituency"—opinion leaders outside the government who have the ear of the administration.

Next the group was asked where they got their information about public opinion. There were no surprises; apparently mail gets a great deal of attention; personal visits to the home lands and talks with the "folks" are valued highly; the vote for and against polls is about even.

Finally the members were asked to cite instances in which public opinion operated, or might have operated to influence policy. Vietnam, not unexpectedly, was the outstanding case, but also mentioned were Cambodia, facts about the CIA, and the Cuban missile crisis.

All in all, one might conclude that in its attitudes and sentiments in international matters, the Congress does not differ greatly from the people.

Text

(1) *Do you consider an informed public opinion vital to a sound foreign policy?*

There were 17 "yes" answers. For examples:

McGovern: Yes, it may be inevitable that public officials with foreign-policy responsibilities tend to misperceive the reasons why we are involved in international affairs and to regard foreign policy as an end in itself rather than as no more than an instrument of domestic military, political, and economic security. An informed populace can be one very healthy restraint on that tendency. Further, diplomacy can never be effective beyond the level of public support for its results, whether it involves a security commitment, a military agreement, an aid program, or an economic arrangement. Public understanding is thus an essential element of successful diplomacy.

Muskie: There is no doubt in my mind that an informed public opinion is vital to a sound and effective foreign policy in a democracy.

On the other side, J. Herbert Burke answered a flat no, and Jonathan Bingham said it was "not vital, but useful."

(2) *In your view, how well informed is the American public?*

Bingham: In an absolute sense, very poorly informed; relative to the public in other countries, quite well-informed.

Broomfield: The American public has an ever-increasing amount of information available (much of it conflicting) from news media and special-interest organizations. The problem for the public is to assimilate the material in order to arrive at an informed opinion.

Burke: As well as the media cover news events.

Case: In comparison with many countries, I believe the American public is pretty well-informed. It seems to me that on a particular issue, public opinion builds slowly and sudden shifts are rare. This is fortunate, since public opinion is certainly essential to the success of long-range policies.

Church: Pretty well informed on major issues.

Derwinski: Reasonably well informed on European issues. Not at all well informed on Latin American, Asian, and African issues.

duPont: Moderately. Need to get out more in-depth information, so that alternatives and their consequences are clearly understood.

Fascell: Relatively well informed.

Findley: Probably better informed than ever before in history. But the need for public information is more critical today than ever before. Is the public well informed? Frankly, I don't feel that I am well informed enough myself.

Fountain: Poorly about foreign policy directions.

Fraser: To paraphrase FDR, we should never underestimate the intelligence of the people nor overestimate the information they possess concerning public affairs.

Gilman: The average citizen is not well informed.

Harrington: It seems to me that the American public is quite poorly informed concerning U.S. foreign policy.

McGovern: I think the Vietnam experience has lessened the tendency of the population to pay less heed to international issues than to domestic questions that affect them more directly. We are short of the ideal, but I find a fairly widespread understanding of international issues, and a mounting sophistication, in discussions with people who are not professionally involved in foreign policy or related fields. As a whole, the American people have a growing sensitivity to the fact that our international conduct can have dramatic consequences for our condition at home.

Pell: Probably better informed than ever before, thanks particularly to TV news coverage and feature programs that have outreach to regions where other public media are less informative on foreign affairs.

Sparkman: I believe the American public is better informed than most people believe. I feel, however, that they want, and are entitled to, additional information as it develops.

Symington: Not too well informed.

Wolfe: Not very well.

(3) *What can be done to inform public opinion?*

Bingham: Higher quality TV, radio, and press.

Broomfield: The principal channel is the news media which, recognizing that responsibility, must continually strive for accuracy and objectivity. Public officials in the Congress and the Executive branch make a contribution, but even here, the extent to which their ideas reach the public depends largely upon the media.

Case: There is usually a long period of "education" before a consensus emerges, for example, the issue of medicare, which in a different form was first proposed by Truman and did not come before the Senate until Eisenhower's second term. The education, of course, takes many forms—covering of special conferences whose findings and conclusions may lead to executive or legislative proposals, hearings in the Congress, press and radio-TV reports and features, efforts by organizations and, most important, personal involvement. In the case of Vietnam, TV coverage was especially influential in bringing about the change in the country's attitude toward withdrawal of American troops.

Church: Good newspapers are best. TV feature news programs also help.

Derwinski: More straight news and historical background reporting, less editorializing, and less emphasis on personalities in foreign-policy news reports.

duPont: More in-depth reporting, but understandable to laymen.

Fascell: Increased educational studies; institutional and issue groups, pro and con; and widest possible dissemination of critical examination by nonspecial interest groups, of bilateral, regional, and international issues; and more participation in people-to-people programs.

Findley: The House committee helps by expanding its role of probing and challenging and investigating.

Fountain: Honest reporting of facts by all media and public educational programs by experts in the field and more openness by the President and Department of State.

Fraser: Daily newspapers and other communications media can devote more of their space to reporting international events that affect the U.S. and give more emphasis to the interdependence of humankind.

Gilman: More public forums, debates, and open hours.

Harrington: The media seem to me to be the most effective but underutilized means of informing the American public about foreign-policy questions. Unfortunately, brief descriptions of international crises too often appear more newsworthy than lengthy, substantive, background articles; as a result, the public is forced to guess as to the reasons for certain policy decisions.

McGovern: The media have a vitally important role, and in recent years they have been fulfilling it much more effectively, both in regular news reports and in occasional special features. To complement that improvement, I think more of the government's foreign-policy business should be conducted in the open. For example, we have frequent briefings in the Foreign Relations Committee from Secretary Kissinger and other Administration personnel—an improvement in itself over earlier practices. Yet these briefings are generally conducted in secret. Of course, privacy with respect to negotiating strategy is sometimes essential, but most of these discussions could easily be held in public without compromising our diplomatic position.

Pell: Expand what is being done now with the public media, especially in the field of public educational TV, and show that developments in other parts of the world increasingly have a direct and practical impact on our daily lives at home; and that in an increasingly interdependent world, the conduct of foreign affairs is more than of academic or passing interest to the average American because it can affect him right down to the kind of car he drives and the purity of the air he breathes.

Sparkman: Use should be made of the news media and through action of individuals in writing articles, letters to the editor, etcetera.

Symington: Less unnecessary secrecy.

Wolfe: Much more education, and seeing to it that foreign policy is opened up to public scrutiny.

(4) *In formulating moves in foreign policy, how much account of public opinion is taken by the Executive and the Congress?*

Bingham: A great deal by the Congress; less by the Executive, except in election years.

Broomfield: A great deal. The House is especially responsive to public opinion.

Burke: Congressmen take their constituents' opinion into account to a great extent, trying very hard to keep their support, as do those in the Executive branch.

Case: Public opinion is very much in the forefront of congressional thinking, but attempts to dissect the interaction get one into "which comes first—the chicken or the egg" discussions. Our sources of information are varied. Constituents are generally free with advice by letter and in person.

Church: Congress has been the most sensitive in recent years.

Derwinski: Secretary Kissinger is obviously indifferent to public opinion. This presents President Ford with one of his major problems. Since individual Congressmen do reflect local public opinion, the Congress as a whole is influenced by grass-roots thinking on foreign policy.

duPont: Some weight is given to public opinion in Congress.

Fascell: Less by the executive, much more by the Congress, although both branches do consider public opinion.

Findley: The response is direct and substantial. Public opinion, through the Congress, forced an end to the Vietnam war, brought curtailment of aid to Cambodia, caused the war-powers resolution to be enacted.

Fountain: To the extent known, it is considered, but the President and the Congress often must avoid political decisions in such areas, especially if the public is not adequately informed.

Fraser: The Executive and the Congress listen to the foreign-policy constituency—those opinion leaders outside of government who are informed and concerned about foreign-policy matters. At the same time, the executive has great influence with the U.S. people in foreign policy and has freedom in this area not always granted in the domestic areas. The Congress, by its nature, usually finds Executive initiatives acceptable. It, perhaps, is more responsive to public opinion than the executive, and less inclined to challenge either public opinion or the executive.

Gilman: Congress gives a great deal of weight to public opinion.

Harrington: The Congress, as well as the Administration, have shown themselves to be quite susceptible to strong lobbying efforts by various special-interest groups. In this fashion, one could conceivably argue that a form of public opinion is taken into account; however, the situation would be greatly improved by a large injection of informed public opinion that would offer a valuable and insightful critique of Executive and Congressional foreign-policy actions.

McGovern: In most cases public opinion is very hard to discern. But in cases where we can discover a dominant view, it weighs quite heavily. I suspect that is more true of the Legislative branch than the Executive, because the smaller and more specific constituencies of a Congressman or Senator are more likely to focus on a small range of issues in expressing their approval or disapproval of his record.

Muskie: Obviously, the formation of policy should not be a simple matter of reacting to public-opinion data, but public opinion does establish certain limits within which a statesman must forge a coherent policy.

Pell: As the elected representatives of the people, the Congress is much more responsive than the Executive in foreign-policy formation. In recent administrations, the Executive branch has tended to ignore the public-opinion factor in foreign-policy decisions, much to its detriment. The approach to the Vietnam war by both the Republican and Democratic administrations is sadly illustrative of this aberration. It is a direct result of the isolation of the President and other administration leaders from the impact of public opinion and indirectly by failure to give Congress, as the American people's elective body, a greater voice in determining foreign-policy decisions before they are pronounced by the Executive branch.

Sparkman: I believe that public opinion is a tremendous force with both the Executive and the Congress.

Symington: Not much.

Wolfe: I do think public opinion has a meaningful influence; however, influence is felt rather slowly—more so in the Congress (which is more responsive).

(5) *Where do you get your information about public opinion—local, national, international? How much attention do you pay to polls?*

Bingham: I get information about my constituents' opinions directly from them, in chance encounters, at meetings, from mail and annual questionnaires. As for national and international public opinion, I get my information largely from the media, especially the *New York Times,* and from occasional trips. I read polls with interest—and with reservations.

Broomfield: Constituent mail and polls of my Congressional district are good barometers of public opinions. National polls and reliable reports of opinions in other countries are also important.

Burke: From the news media—and it is taken with a grain of salt.

Church: From all sources, including polls.

Derwinski: From selected publications, government reports, correspondence with business experts and respected academicians. I pay very little attention to polls.

duPont: From my district correspondence and contacting additional publications. I don't pay attention to polls.

Fascell: All media, Congressional hearings, mail, personal contacts, polls.

Findley: I read polls but consider thoughtful unsolicited mail from average citizens a better guide. I take annual surveys of my constituents. The best polling is direct, and for that reason I welcome travel opportunities and pump everyone I meet.

Fountain: All media—as much as I can read.

Fraser: Both local and national polls. I don't ignore the polls.

Gilman: I base my information on public opinion; upon polls, which I take periodically; town hall meetings; and citizens' advisory committees in my district.

McGovern: Information comes through just about every kind of communication—mail, conversations, news reports, and countless other contacts. Polls are one of many sources and, like other sources, they have clearly recognized weaknesses. Questionnaires are seldom sufficiently comprehensive to reach underlying attitudes, and the results therefore tend to be quite transitory. Certainly everyone in public life watches polls, but usually as no more than one way of evaluating how the American people are likely to respond to developments over the longer term.

Pell: The best guide to public opinion is from the reaction, or lack of it, not only from constituents but from the country as a whole, through mail and oral contacts. Reaction in the public media, including public polls, is also valuable, especially in providing a benchmark by which to evaluate expressions of public opinion received directly.

Sparkman: As to local opinion, I rely heavily upon mail from my constituents. As to national opinion, I follow carefully the various polls that may be taken by national polling groups, also upon the news media. For international opinion, I follow closely the reporting and writing of representatives of the media in the foreign countries and also upon the statements of experts in the different parts of the world.

Symington: From all possible sources.

Wolfe: I do not pay much attention to polls. Listen to media and mail.

(6) *Can you give instances in which public opinion influenced policy and others in which an informed opinion might have prevented mistakes in foreign policy?*

Bingham: Public opinion certainly influenced policy on the Vietnam war. An informed opinion might well have prevented the U.S. from getting involved in Vietnam to begin with.

Broomfield: Public opinion in the United States was the key factor in the actions of Congress in passing the war powers bill and later overriding the President's veto. More recently, public opinion played a major role in the action taken by Congress to cut off aid to Turkey over the Greek-Turkey-Cyprus dispute.

Burke: Our foreign aid programs have been influenced by public opinion, and there have been many mistakes because of a lack of affirmative opinion.

Church: Public opinion finally forced an end to our part in the war in Vietnam.

Derwinski: The debate in the Congress over the Cyprus crisis and U.S. relations between Greece and Turkey were clearly influenced by public opinion. In a consistent manner, U.S. Middle East policy has obviously been influenced by public opinion. A public that tired of the Vietnam war certainly influenced foreign-policy changes there.

duPont: In the case of the Jackson/Vanilo trade amendment—Jewish opinion forced passage of the amendment. Informed, balanced reporting might have prevented the error.

Fascell: Vietnam, Middle East, Cyprus, détente with Russia and China, Cuba; indeed, any other trouble spot or problem involving foreign policy.

Findley: Had the Pentagon papers been reported sooner, the war, I believe, would have ended sooner. NATO has had a steady decline due largely to lack of informed public opinion.

Fountain: In the Vietnam war our uninformed public and dishonest President made the situation difficult.

Fraser: Vietnam, in answer to both parts of the question. Our policy on Soviet Jewry has been influenced by public opinion. I feel that all policies can be improved by responding to informed public opinion.

Gilman: Public opinion influenced the Congress to limit our nation's full involvement in Vietnam.

McGovern: I think Vietnam qualifies on both counts. An informed citizenry, with a greater understanding of the issues involved might well have prevented our deep involvement in the war. And it was a better-informed populace that eventually forced the termination of our involvement.

Muskie: The best recent example of public opinion forcing a change in foreign policy was, in my view, the Vietnam War. I have little doubt that the Nixon Administration would have preferred extending our involvement had not public opinion—and the approaching election—convinced them otherwise.

Pell: I think the way the country rallied around the Administration in the Cuban missile crisis influenced the President in adopting a firm, cool policy that led to the USSR blinking first in the eyeball-to-eyeball confrontation. On the other hand, had the various administrations involved taken the public into their confidence as to whether we should intervene—and if so, how—in Vietnam, the country could have been spared the tragic errors that cost us so much in blood, treasure, and national unity. By our going into the Vietnam war massively through the back door, the public never received an adequate explanation of our objectives or the opportunity of open discussion of other alternatives to the course actually followed. Greater Congressional debate of these alternatives would have been particularly helpful in avoiding some of the pitfalls into which the Executive branch fell.

Symington: Laos, Cambodia; less troops in Europe; more knowledge of CIA functioning; nuclear force.

Wolfe: Vietnam on both counts.

QUESTIONNAIRE 3

To Authors in Field of Public Opinion

The questionnaire was answered by the following:

William Crotty, Professor of Political Science, Northwestern University

Leonard Doob, Professor of Psychology, Yale University

Lloyd Free, President, Institute of International Social Research

Charles Glock, Professor of Sociology, University of California

Doris Graber, Professor of Political Science, University of Illinois

David Riesman, Professor of Sociology, Harvard University

James Rosenau, Director, Institute of Transnational Studies, University of Southern California

Rita Simon, Professor of Communications, University of Illinois

Sidney Verba, Professor of Government, Harvard University

Summary

The editors thought it was a bright idea to have from authors of books on public opinion their definitions of the theme of their works. But we came upon little illumination in that group also. Five found any definition unsatisfactory; the others offered generalized observations, proving once more that public opinion is not one thing but many.

No one of the authors who responded is completely satisfied with the polls. Most feel that inasmuch as they are the only system we have, they will have to do until we devise something better. Some respondents are inclined to discount them on crucial points, because the questions are not well phrased or the value of the answers is insufficiently appraised.

There is a strong belief, however, that refinements in the polls are possible. Especially it is suggested that information questions be asked so that the pollers can appraise the value of the responses. Also, there is a warning that the polls should be questioned because they may be put out for political purposes and may be deliberately misleading. The good pollsters would probably welcome what in effect would be a "pure polls act," but the opposition would be potent and there would be a lot of talk about the First Amendment.

In answer to the question about the sources of their information about public opinion, the polls are, of course, discussed, but only as one factor.

Therefore, in addition to the polls, the opinion analysts watch and read the media in order to measure the depth of feelings and take into account background and general attitude, which are often more important than the answers given to the stock questions. In other words, they take full account of what is the indubitable fact that most so-called opinion is not opinion at all (which denotes thought and logic) but sheer emotion.

Text

(1) *How do you define public opinion?*

Crotty: I think of public opinion in empirical terms— who holds what views, on what issues, with what degree of intensity. I think it is a subtle, fractionated distribution of impulses (responses for or against with some—although not much—substantive content). I believe you begin to arrive at what is more commonly thought of as "public opinion" when you begin to aggregate the variety of individual views, generalizing and simplifying somewhat, and emphasizing the common tendencies (rather than their discrete properties). Once this is done, you can speak of broad sets of opinions held by various groupings within the society and you can begin to match these with party choices, leadership policies, and even legislative outcomes (allowing for inferences along the way).

Doob: To try to answer your questions, I have pulled out that old book of mine to which you refer. I still agree with the simple definition I proposed in italics on p. 35, but with this difference: I now think neither the definition nor the term itself is very helpful. That definition, however, foreshadows my present conviction: it is much more fruitful to discover or analyze the attitudes, beliefs, values, etcetera of specific groups within a society than to refer to public opinion. In short, the term, I think, has become a somewhat tricky metaphor.

Graber: I like to define *public opinion* as publicly expressed views about current issues of wide public concern, held by representative groups of people and presumably derived from public discussion of these issues.

The essential elements of this definition are that (a) the views must be publicly expressed, rather than being silent beliefs, or views expressed privately to small audiences; (b) the subject matter must concern issues of current saliency, rather than long-standing basic philosophical tenets or ideologies; (c) the issues must be important enough to potentially garner the attention of large segments of the population (though by no means the entire American public);

(d) the people who hold these views must appear to be representative of the publics most likely to be concerned with these issues; and (e) the views must originate through some process of consensus-creation, which involves sharing of information and evaluations among the members of the group.

On any issue, there may be a variety of public opinions held by a variety of publics. This gives political leaders a chance to choose those publics whose claims they allegedly heed in fulfillment of democratic obligations.

Rosenau: I do not think there is any single definition of public opinion that is appropriate. Much depends on which segments of the public, with respect to what kinds of activities they undertake, that one is talking about. In addition, one has to distinguish between passive members of the public who respond to the questions of pollsters and the active members of the public who have structured opinions on which they act.

Simon: I would define public opinion as James Bryce did, "the aggregate of views men (people) hold regarding matters that affect or interest the community."

Verba: Public opinion is, of course, very difficult to define, which is perhaps why many students of the subject do not define it. I suppose that in some general way the term refers to the set of attitudes or opinions on public matters held by the citizenry. As we know, there are different "publics" for different issues that hold opinions with different levels of intensity. And it is this aspect of public opinion that deserves the closest study. In fact, my general impression has been from a variety of political studies that any time one attempts to use a single summary statistic (an average, a single percentage having a particular characteristic, etc.) to characterize a complex population such as that in the United States, one has produced a serious distortion. In almost all cases, what counts are the internal variations.

(2) *Are you satisfied with present methods of determining public opinion?*

Crotty: No; I think the present studies of public opinion only begin to scratch the surface of an extraordinarily complex subject. The methods (or methodologies) per se are not at fault. I believe the weaknesses are in the conceptualization (and to a lesser degree execution) of the studies. Our measurements at present are fairly rudimentary (but hopefully improving).

Doob: I am not satisfied with the methods we use or even those we might use to measure the phenomena presumably subsumed by the term. One problem, however, has obviously been solved: the theory, and to a lesser degree, the technique of sampling. What we would always like to have is an analysis in depth of the respondents' attitudes and beliefs, and indeed that might be achieved if we had the time and energy to spend probing in the manner of a psychiatrist. This is obviously impractical, since a large sample has to be surveyed. I do not think we have the techniques quickly and validly to ascertain the stability and importance of what individuals assert when they are suddenly questioned by a pollster. To a certain extent, therefore, we have all been misled a trifle when the generally excellent forecasting of election returns by the polls (a rather simple task, at least in a democracy) inclines us to accord them more general reliability and validity.

Free: As to sound ways to measure public opinion, I am half-way satisfied with the current methods used by the better polling organizations. I would add, however, that a great many questions are customarily asked the public which they have no competence to answer because of sheer ignorance on the part of a considerable proportion as to the issues involved. For example, in my *Political Beliefs of Americans* study, it turned out that one-quarter of the national cross-section had never even heard or read of NATO, the then keystone of our international policies, and an equal proportion did not even know that the government of Mainland China was Communist!

At a sheerly technical level, therefore, I feel it incumbent on the polls to ask far more questions about information and knowledge in order to rate respondents in terms of how well informed they are about what is being asked.

Beyond this, I feel that the polls customarily do a once-over-lightly, skimming job in testing sometimes ambivalent attitudes, as distinguished from using a battery of questions to get at all aspects of the matter. The contrast between ideological and operational attitudes is an example.

Graber: I am not satisfied with present methods of determining public opinion but see little chance of any major changes in the near future. My dissatisfaction springs from two separate basic yet related problems. One is the difficulty of measuring public opinion adequately, which has seriously crippled public opinion research. The second is the fact that many political leaders, laymen and even scholars divine public opinion through unscientific methods, conducive to producing errors that will warp judgments about public opinions. As mentioned earlier, inaccurate appraisals are compounded by deliberately false appraisals that are made to serve political purposes.

The principal measurement difficulties lie in adequate sampling of various publics concerned with particular issues. The national samples used by various polling organizations are far too crude in their selection of respondents and in their methods of questioning them and interpreting the responses in the light of important personal and political background factors. We have much of the technical know-how to do a better job, but we lack the money.

Rosenau: As for your question of whether I am satisfied with present methods of determining it, one is of course never satisfied, although I think great methodological strides have been made in recent years by a number of different scholars.

Simon: The usual method of determining public opinion is by taking a poll. But the typical poll or survey fails to take into account the hierarchical nature of society; the fact that there are different strata in the society, the fact that society is organized into all sorts of interest groups, et cetera. The simplistic view of society that is implied by survey analysis is the greatest source of dissatisfaction to me. Polls are, of course, extremely useful for voting studies, in which there is a one-man-one-vote situation, but I think there are many problems when one tries to interpret or predict public sentiment on domestic and foreign-policy issues on the basis of poll data.

Verba: As for the methods of determining public opinion, I am a great fan of systematic survey research if it is used with care and qualification. It is one of the most powerful tools in the social sciences, and has reached levels of great sophistication when it comes to sampling and the like. I think that the two major problems with systematic surveys as a means of eliciting public attitudes are the fact that one receives answers only to the questions one has asked and one often ignores the problems of internal diversity and intensity. We know quite well how to standardize and improve samples. There are no standard and "objective" techniques for developing questions. Thus, one often sees people responding to public opinion results as if they reflected a God-given truth rather than the responses to a particular set of questions.

(3) *When you seek light on any phase of polling, to what sources do you turn?*

Crotty: I think polls represent a gross distortion of views, so open to abuse as to be taken with some skepticism. Even the most reputable pollsters are subject to lapses that are unfortunate. I look to the vote. Curiously, I am a great believer in the efficacy of the vote and despite the great difficulty at times in fathoming its meaning, I feel it is a significant, decisive, and measurable statement of an individual's political views.

Second, I look to reanalyses of data taken from academic surveys (such as those conducted by Warren Miller's Center for Political Studies at the University of Michigan).

Doob: Of course, I consult the polls whenever the data

are available; they are always better than sagacious guesses, even by journalists. But I simultaneously add a stiff dose of skepticism, for I know how suddenly shifts occur. Another important ingredient, I think, must be historical and anthropological analyses, for they give us insight—again with a margin of error—into what individuals are likely to feel or believe at a given moment. It is likewise important to know something about the content of the mass media, though here too the interpretation is not straightforward: what they communicate reflects and affects the views of their audience and it is very tricky at a given moment to know at what point you are on this spiral.

Free: Frankly, I think the most promising route not only for getting at attitudes, but for providing some understanding and explanation of them, is a combination of the customary type of polling, combined with depth or semi-depth probing within the framework of the larger sample. This has proved very useful to me in some of my political studies in which I have supplemented the polling operation with intensive interviews conducted by a psychiatrist friend of mine, who has been attempting to apply psychiatric techniques in the field of national and international issues.

Graber: My own prescription for measuring public opinion calls for using as many indicators as possible in any particular case. For instance, if I undertook a study of public opinion on the issue of amnesty for Vietnam deserters, I would not be content with examining a series of public opinion polls. I would want to investigate whether the people who voiced their opinions had been exposed to public discussion of the issue and had derived their views from a sound informational base. This might entail a study of the sources of information available to respondents and the uses which they made of these sources. It might involve in-depth explorations of the meanings they placed on the effects of these opinions.

If the focus were placed on the effects of these opinions on policy-makers, it would be necessary first to examine the policy-makers' perceptions of the nature of public opinion on the issue, and then the political context in which these opinions would be considered. The precise combination of factors that I would study would depend on the nature of the questions to be answered, on the availability of data, and on the cost and ease of data collection and analysis.

Riesman: Concerning methods of determining public opinion, I am very much a pluralist. Ever since I was a student of Professor Carl J. Friedrich forty years ago I have read letters in newspapers, and not only the eminent newspapers, inquiries to Ann Landers and other such things also. I listen to what I have come to call talk-jockers on the radio to get a sense of what people are thinking and feeling who are not among the articulate or professional strata. I want to know the tone of voice in which they speak about affairs. I am also interested in what might be called unobtrusive measures of public opinion. The housewives' meat boycott was an illustration, because it was spontaneous and said something about attitudes and expectations; the strikes of the independent truckers had a similar quality. These actions had bearing on what I always think about, namely, the weight of opinion and its location in the social structure; as you know from my writing, I do not believe that each opinion counts for one and no more than one.

Rosenau: One turns to different sources for information and measurement, depending on which segments of the public one is interested in. One might use polls if one is concerned with the mass public, but these of course have to be taken with a grain of salt inasmuch as much of the opinion that the polls elicit does not exist prior to the posing of the question by the interviewer. If one is interested in the active stratum of the society, then one should turn not to polls but to other sources wherein the activity becomes manifest.

Simon: The sources that I think are useful for helping me interpret public opinion are the positions assumed and the statements that are made by different groups or organizations in the society. In foreign policy, for example, I think it is very useful to listen to what spokesmen for various ethnic communities have to say—how often do they say it, to whom, and with what intensity. I think that spokesmen or representatives of organized groups in the society, and the views and opinions that appear in their publications, are more useful sources of public opinion on national issues than are poll data.

Verba: The sources for the study of public opinion are so many and varied that one does not know where to begin. The leading academic journals in political science and sociology contain a large amount of material, as do the popular press and the like. There are also very useful collections of past public-opinion material at the University of Michigan and at Williams College. These, of course, are so large and diverse that one cannot approach them without some specific question in mind.

QUESTIONNAIRE 4

To Managing Editors

The questionnaire to managing editors was designed to discover how much attention was given in the press to international news and the factors that determine the allotment. There were 37 responses.

The average amount of space assigned to foreign news was given as 17%, but it must be kept in mind that the "news hole" includes nonnews features, in fact everything but advertising. So my guess is that the figure is closer to 10%. (On a "newspaper of record" the figure is one-third foreign, one-third national, and one-third local.)

Obviously an inadequate allowance for international news is based on the belief that the interest in foreign news is not great. This is reflected in the response to the second question: "How do you rate the reader interest in foreign news?" The answers were: High—6; Moderate—24; Low—7.

The third question, "On what is this judgment based?", brought a variety of answers: reader surveys, direct contacts, letters to the editor, conversations, gut feeling. My guess is that it's a toss-up between reader surveys (Gallup editing, call it) and gut feeling.

In the fourth question the editors were asked what were their main sources of foreign news. The answers showed these averages: Associated Press, 30%; United Press International, 30%; other sources, 30%; own staff, 10%.

This was the fifth question: How highly do you rate the foreign news supplied to you? The answers: Good, 19 editors; Adequate, 16; Inadequate, 2.

Question #6 was this: Do you think interest in foreign news can be increased by making it more understandable, more relevant, or in any other way? The yes response came from 32; five had reservations, on the general ground that reader interest is the result of life-style.

The final question was whether the respondents considered it important that such interest be increased. The response was a unanimous yes; with the world shrinking in size, an event in any part of it affects all the other parts; the days of isolation are gone forever.